Procrastination

The Practical Step-by-step Guide to Doing Difficult Things Ignoring Distractions Improving

(A Simple Guide to Hacking Laziness and Overcoming Procrastination)

Stephen Martinez

Published By **Regina Loviusher**

Stephen Martinez

All Rights Reserved

Procrastination: The Practical Step-by-step Guide to Doing Difficult Things Ignoring Distractions Improving (A Simple Guide to Hacking Laziness and Overcoming Procrastination)

ISBN 978-1-7750277-8-2

No part of this guidebook shall be reproduced in any form without permission in writing from the publisher except in the case of brief quotations embodied in critical articles or reviews.

Legal & Disclaimer

The information contained in this book is not designed to replace or take the place of any form of medicine or professional medical advice. The information in this book has been provided for educational & entertainment purposes only.

The information contained in this book has been compiled from sources deemed reliable, and it is accurate to the best of the Author's knowledge; however, the Author cannot guarantee its accuracy and validity and cannot be held liable for any errors or omissions. Changes are periodically made to this book. You must consult your doctor or get professional medical advice before using any of the suggested remedies, techniques, or information in this book.

Upon using the information contained in this book, you agree to hold harmless the Author from and against any damages, costs, and expenses, including any legal fees potentially resulting from the application of any of the information provided by this guide. This disclaimer applies to any damages or injury caused by the use and application, whether directly or indirectly, of any advice or information presented, whether for breach of contract, tort, negligence, personal injury, criminal intent, or under any other cause of action.

You agree to accept all risks of using the information presented inside this book. You need to consult a professional medical practitioner in order to ensure you are both able and healthy enough to participate in this program.

Table Of Contents

Chapter 1: The Concept Of Procrastination 1

Chapter 2: The Procrastination-Productivity Cycle 11

Chapter 3: Setting Clear Goals And Priorities 22

Chapter 4: Overcoming Procrastination Through Self-Discipline 32

Chapter 5: Cultivating Motivation And Inspiration... 45

Chapter 6: Boosting Creativity And Innovation... 64

Chapter 7: Navigating Procrastination In The Digital Age 76

Chapter 8: Creating An Environment For Productivity 94

Chapter 9: Embracing A Procrastination-Free Future 105

Chapter 10: Procrastination The Art Of Delay.. 110

Chapter 11: Understanding Procrastination 118

Chapter 12: Instantly Stop Procrastination Technique (Ispt) 127

Chapter 13: Step-By-Step Guide........... 136

Chapter 14: Tools And Resources To Support.. 144

Chapter 15: Common Pitfalls And How To Overcome Them 152

Chapter 16: Strengthening Your Willpower And Discipline 159

Chapter 17: Success Stories Real-Life Implementations................................... 166

Chapter 18: Frequently Asked Questions 173

Chapter 19: The Path Forward 178

Chapter 1: The Concept Of Procrastination

This dimly illuminated space the blank page was staring back at me on the screen of my computer. The cursor was blinking constantly in mockery of my inability to begin typing. "I'll start in just a few minutes," I considered. However, those moments turned into hours as the deadline was getting closer. It wasn't the only time that I've been caught by the tyranny of delay. What did I not know was that the seemingly simple habit was actually an intricate and fascinating nature and was deeply embedded in the intricate mind of all brains?

1.1 The Nature of Procrastination

The act of procrastination, which is like a hidden force is often able to sneak through our lives without being, noticed This isn't just an excuse to put things off, it's about balancing your current desires and future goals. There's been a time when we've tried telling ourselves we'll begin working out, studying, or tackling that dream idea "tomorrow." However, why is it that tomorrow doesn't seem to show up?

Procrastination refers to the practice of putting off actions seem to be difficult or burdensome, and choosing the immediate enjoyment instead. In the moment, pleasure from watching another show on television show or browsing social media may easily overshadow the joy of finishing an assignment. The tendency to prioritize the pleasure of a short-term fix over the long-term benefit can lead to a continuous battle.

1.2 The Psychology behind Procrastination

The mind is a complex landscape filled with emotions, thoughts and motives. This is where procrastination is a breeding ground. In the heart of this puzzle is the interaction with our brain's prefrontal cortex as well as the limbic system.

The prefrontal cortex acts as our rational central point, responsible for deciding plans, controlling our impulses. This is the part of us which knows that we need to start this task now, rather than watch another show. However, it is often fighting our limbic system which is the part of the brain that controls emotions, seeking pleasure, and is resistant to pain. This conflict between both emotional and cognitive factors makes the ideal setting that allows procrastination to flourish.

1.3 Why Do We Procrastinate?

Humans have the instinct to search for ease and avoid discomfort. This instinctive urge, previously an evolutionary mechanism for survival, today results in procrastination. Fear of failing, anxiety about failure, perfectionists, as well as a lack of a clear goal can contribute to the procrastination we do.

The fear of failure: Fear of failing in a job can make us feel overwhelmed. It's more convenient to defer beginning than risking our confidence in ourselves and ego.

The fear of success the process of achieving success brings about change which can be scary. A leap into the unknown regardless of a good outcome may result in the urge to delay.

In pursuit of perfection could cause a fearful feeling of failing to meet standard requirements. In reality, this fear causes people to avoid starting even.

A lack of clear Goals In the absence of clearly-defined goals It can be difficult to identify motivation. Inconsistency in what is required to be completed may lead to delays.

1.4 The Costs of Procrastination

While it is tempting as it can be to postpone things it is true that the consequences of procrastination can be significant, and are often concealed just beneath the skin. It erodes confidence in ourselves and can lead to a spiral of guilt and stress. As we put off in our process, the more stressed we become about the deadline that is approaching. When the day finally comes for us to take on the challenge we feel guilt which further effects the mental health of us.

In addition, procrastination creates consequences for our personal relationships, work and general well-being. The loss of opportunities, the strain on relationships as well as a lower performance can be the cost of accepting this deceitful behavior.

In the next chapters, we'll dive further into the psychology processes at work and look into ways to free ourselves from the shackles of procrastination. However, recognizing what causes procrastination can be the initial step to overcome it. Therefore, let's start the journey of self-discovery, and transformation that takes us out of procrastination's close embrace to a freeing realm of putting our actions into the necessary action today.

Recognizing Procrastination Patterns

For self-development, being aware of one's own can be described as being a beacon that illuminates the road towards progress. When we enter the misty world of putting off work, we need to be equipped with this lamp, shining light at the intricate patterns under the top layer. We can begin this fascinating exploration of discovering the patterns that are often feeding the beast of procrastination.

2.1   Self-Reflection   for   Identifying Procrastination

"Know thyself," the old Greek phrase, has the gold weight in the fight against the habit of procrastination. Looking into the mirror of reflection on ourselves can reveal insight into our habits and allows us to untangle the web of distractions that procrastination has created.

Self-reflection goes beyond looking at the reason we put off work It's about examining our psychological landscape as well as triggers and thinking patterns. Take a look at the time you've slowed down at times in the past. Did you avoid a project due to its difficulty or the fear of failing or because the task wasn't in line with your objectives? Writing down your thoughts can be an opportunity to make changes.

2.2 Common Triggers of Procrastination

Imagine playing a game of dominos One trigger can start an entire chain reaction of procrastination. The process of identifying triggers is as simple as finding the first domino is the first step to stop the chain reaction before it starts.

Perfectionist: Fear of doing something wrong could make us feel insecure. It happens most often when we set unreasonable standards for ourselves.

Incompleteness: If the tasks are not clearly defined or have clear targets, they are reasons for delays. It can become a hazard.

Insanity: The thought of tackling an overwhelming project can lead to avoidance. By breaking it down into manageable, smaller pieces will help ease the anxiety.

Procrastination for negative emotions: It can be an effective way of avoiding negative emotions such as anger, boredom or even frustration. It is a collateral injury.

Inattention: Jobs which don't match our beliefs or interests can be a source of discontent. A lack of motivation may lead to the habit of putting off work for too long.

2.3 Types of Tasks We Often Procrastinate

It doesn't care about the type of task It can infiltrate every aspect of our life. However, some types of jobs appear to be more susceptible to it.

Work-related Tasks: Jobs which require physical or mental effort can trigger the urge to delay. The mind seeks the path that is the least effort.

The monotonous task: repetitive or monotonous activities can seem boring, which is why we put them off in favour of other activities that are more interesting.

Complex tasks: The task of completing many steps could be overwhelming. Complexity can discourage people from even starting.

The unpleasant tasks: Tasks that come to negative or uncomfortable feelings including conflict resolution tend to be avoided because of their undesirable character.

Long-Term Projects: Tasks that take months or even weeks to complete could lead to procrastination due the distant deadlines. It is possible for the illusion of time to cause delays.

2.4 Keeping a Procrastination Journal

Imagine having a trusted partner by your side, keeping track of your adventures through the midst of procrastination. Journals for procrastination serve as a mirror that reflects your habits, triggers as well as your triumphs. If you notice yourself putting off a task note down the project as well as the date and the reason you believe caused the delay.

As time passes it will become apparent that patterns are emerging - an intricate puzzle that is slowly being put into. Do you find yourself constantly avoiding specific types of work or putting off tasks at specific time periods of the each day? This journal will reveal your personal Procrastination Landscape.

When it comes to self-development, self-awareness is the key to change. In bringing our patterns of procrastination to the light, we open the way for an incredibly change. Armed with a better understanding of our triggers, and the tendencies we exhibit and triggers, we can begin a journey which promises to free our lives from the shackles of procrastination. Let's go on this adventure with open minds and open minds, getting always closer to living the life that is full of action and determination.

Chapter 2: The Procrastination-Productivity Cycle

The dance between procrastination, and productiveness is a one that leaves people feeling caught up by a storm of emotions. Imagine this scenario: you are sitting in your chair to begin working on your project and promise yourself you'll begin with just a few minutes. Then, the moment turns into a long time as you find yourself lost among a ocean of distracting thoughts. It's a tale many of us know well - the procrastination-productivity cycle.

3.1 How Procrastination Affects Productivity

Think of that your precious time is a finite resource which you are able to use or invest. Refraining from doing something, which is similar to reckless spending, saps the value of our time and hampers the efficiency of our lives. It's a clever thief who is able to steal not just our hours but also our feelings of satisfaction.

The process begins with a simple idea and you pause to start the task in search of a brief relief from your discomfort. Then you engage in distraction-related tasks, such as browsing video or social media. When time passes worry and guilt begin to creep into your life, and gnawing at your tranquility. The task is finally completed and the pressure to finish the task erodes the level of the task. Feeling exhausted and dissatisfied, swear to yourself that the next time you will do better but then you discover yourself caught up again in the same cycle.

3.2 Breaking Down the Cycle Step by Step

The procrastination-productivity cycle thrives on its meticulously designed steps, each one leading seamlessly into the next. Let's unravel some of the layers that make up this complicated process to better understand the underlying mechanisms:

Step 1: Avoiding Tasks This process usually begins with an apparent thought, "I'll start in a little while." This is a temptation that we readily accept, delaying any action in exchange for a momentary sense of peace.

Step 2: Distractions and Gratification: To get some relief from the stress of the upcoming task We turn towards distractions such as the internet, entertainment or whatever activity provides instant satisfaction. The momentary distraction provides the dopamine rush that bolsters your behavior.

Step 3: Anxiety and Guilt When the deadline gets closer, feelings of guilt and fear appear. It's clear how much amount of time that we've wasted as well as the need for action to be completed. The emotions drive us into a state abstention.

Step 4: Unstable action: As the pressure builds it is finally time to start the work. The time pressure requires us to rush into the process. Quality of work is hampered, resulting in feelings of unsatisfaction.

5. Relaxation and Reward: After your task is completed There is a brief sense of relief can

be felt. It's a brief moment of respite that acts as a positive reinforcement to the procrastination behaviour, which strengthens the pattern.

3.3 The Role of Motivation in Breaking the Cycle

Motivation is the secret ingredient that has the power to disrupt the procrastination-productivity cycle. Think of motivation as a shining figure, which illuminates the path to efficiency. When we're really driven, we skip all the first steps of the cycle and immediately get to work.

Finding out what motivates you is essential. Motivation is intrinsically derived from individual values, interests and satisfaction that you get from your work. External motivation is derived through external influences like rewards as well as recognition. It can also be a way to prevent the negative effects.

To end the cycle it is necessary to harness the force of motivation:

Create meaningful goals Set clear goals and the reasons why they are important to you. This will help you tap into your own intrinsic desire to succeed, and creates a firm basis for your actions.

The Chunk Method: Divide the tasks down into manageable, smaller chunks. This helps to counter the overwhelming feelings which can lead to procrastination.

Design a Rewards System by combining tasks with reward. It bridges the gap between pleasure for a short time and goals for the long term.

Do Self-Compassion Practice: Be gentle with yourself, particularly when you fall into the vicious cycle. Self-compassion reduces the negative feelings and re-invigorates you to take actions.

"Imagine Success": Think of your sense of satisfaction which comes from completing your task. Visualization fuels your motivation.

In the complex choreography of the procrastination-productivity cycle, motivation is the music that guides our steps. Once we are able to dance in this direction and move closer to movement and away from the grip of the procrastination cycle. It's not always a straight line However, with knowledge of how the cycle works it is easier to maneuver the turn-by-turns.

Continue on the path of exploration, in which each step we take leads us one step closer to breaking from the cycle and moving towards the life that is purposeful.

Overcoming Procrastination: A Mindset Shift

In the midst of all the complexities of personal growth is a powerful thread that can be transformed - the power of our mindset. Our minds, nimble and durable are the most important factor in liberating ourselves from the shackles of procrastination. The chapter we're in will go in a process of changing our perceptions, and forming the mindset that not just eliminates procrastination, but also opens the way to growth and taking action.

4.1 Cultivating a Growth Mindset

Imagine a beautiful garden, cultivated with love, where every seed is able to grow into something wonderful. The same way, our minds as they are nurtured by a positive mentality, can turn challenges into potential opportunities.

The term "growth mindset" refers to an understanding that skills and abilities can be improved by effort, education, and persistence. It's a way to counter the fixed-minded mindset that holds that abilities and characteristics are inherent and cannot be changed.

Achieving a positive mindset includes:

Accepting Challenges: Instead of abstaining from challenges look at them as an opportunity for development. They are the stones which shape our capabilities.

Insisting Despite Setbacks: Instead of instead of being demotivated by the failures consider them to be stepping steps towards achievement. Every setback can be a valuable lesson.

The path towards Mastery: Be aware the importance of a consistent effort throughout long periods of. Hard work and dedication make the way to perfection.

Learn from Criticism Instead of avoiding critics, accept criticism as an opportunity to grow. Feedback constructively is a compass that points towards growth.

4.2 Embracing Imperfectionism

In a society that praises perfection, accepting imperfection is a form of resistance in a way of stating that the pace of advancement is more important than perfection.

The desire to be perfect often leads to procrastination, due to the fear that being unable to meet the standards of perfection could cripple our. Accepting imperfections shifts our attention away from our goal to the journey and shifts our focus from perfect result to meaningful improvement.

Recognize that mistakes can be learning Opportunity: Mistakes should not be seen as indicators of failure. They are an opportunity to improve. Every mistake is an opportunity to improve and learn.

Recognize Progress over Perfection Do not wait for perfectionism, be proud of your progress throughout the process. Small wins can lead to huge successes.

Reframe Failure: Failure isn't an end in itself, it's just an opportunity to take a different path towards successful. Each loss contributes to the growth story of your business.

4.3 The Power of Positive Self-Talk

Imagine having a person whispering affirmations in your ear informing you of your strengths and value. This is your own inner voice. Positive self-talk is a potent tool against indecision.

The negative self-talk that we make about ourselves often leads to self-doubt and the tendency to delay. The self-talk tells us that we aren't competent enough, intelligent enough or competent enough. The shift to self-talk that is positive could change our perspective:

Beware of Negative Thoughts: If you find yourself thinking negative thoughts you should challenge your beliefs. Find facts that support or debunk your negative thinking.

Utilize affirmations to create positive affirmations to counteract doubts about yourself. Be sure to repeatedly affirm your strengths and capabilities. your strengths.

Adopt Self-Compassion You should treat yourself with the same compassion you'd show a person you love. Instead of criticizing yourself for delay, be patient and offer encourage yourself.

Visualize your success: Visualizing yourself finishing an assignment successfully will boost your motivation and confidence. The visualisation helps you visualize the picture of the outcome you want to achieve.

As you journey through the shifting mental state, keep in mind that changing requires time. Like a tree that grows stronger with every passing season, your attitude evolves by conscious effort and consistent repetition. cultivating a growth mindset accepting imperfectionism as well as adopting positive self-talk, can not just assist you in conquering procrastination, but can also help you become an empowered, self-confident person. When you accept these changes and build the basis to live a life that is full of action that will lead to growth and change.

Chapter 3: Setting Clear Goals And Priorities

The vast web of self-improvement making goals and prioritizing your tasks is the process of transforming intentions into actions. Imagine yourself standing on the edges of an expansive area, carrying maps that chart your path to achieving your goals. The chapter we're discussing will dive deep into setting specific goals, separating the important and urgent tasks as well as creating the task structure that leads you to the right path for success.

5.1 The Importance of Well-Defined Goals

They are the mainstays that help us navigate through the world. They give direction, a purpose as well as a feeling of achievement. The goals that are well-defined are beacons that help to illuminate the path ahead and clearing the cloud of uncertainty.

Clarity Breeds commitment: When your objectives are clear the commitment you have to achieve the goals grows. In contrast, uncertainty however can allow procrastination to creep through.

The importance of guidance in the midst of constant distractions, goals serve like compasses to help us stay in the right direction. When you're in a position to wander to the side, you'll be reminded by your goals of the destination you're trying to reach.

Measurable Milestones: An established target is quantifiable. You can monitor your progress and then celebrate every accomplishment.

Improved Focus: Goals help you clarity in the midst of chaos. They remove unnecessary activities and help you focus on important things.

5.2 Differentiating Between Urgent and Important Tasks

Think of a list of tasks as landscape - certain jobs are bursting with plants that enhance the beauty of your garden, while other tasks include invasive weeds that hinder development. The distinction between important and urgent chores is a skill that can be learned by tending this particular garden to nurture those things that are truly important.

Urgent Tasks: urgent assignments require urgent attention because of imminent deadlines or other pressures. These tasks are often seen as crucial, however they may not match your long-term objectives.

Important Tasks: These jobs directly impact your goals over time as well as your values and general wellbeing. They aren't always accompanied by pressing deadlines, but they have a lasting impact.

It's the Eisenhower Matrix: This matrix categorizes work into four types crucial and urgent essential however not essential, important, but not crucial not urgent or crucial. This tool helps identify tasks that need to be prioritized.

Reduce Reactive Behavior: Concentrating exclusively on the urgent task can put us in a state of reactivity that is constantly reacting to demands from outside. The priority of important work puts the focus on taking a proactive approach and drives our actions towards our objectives.

5.3 Creating a Personalized Task Hierarchy

Think of each task as an element of a puzzle that contributes to the overall view of your daily life. The process of creating a customized work hierarchy is about arranging the pieces in a manner that is compatible with your ideals objectives, priorities, and goals.

Find Your Values: Your beliefs serve as the compass through which you make your choices. Make sure that your work is aligned to these values and you will experience satisfaction and satisfaction.

Long-Term in contrast to. Short-Term: Separate your tasks into both short and long-term groups. This will prevent the lure of a quick fix from obscuring the importance of long-term objectives.

Break tasks into steps The task of tackling a large amount can become too overwhelming and cause the tendency to delay. Reduce them down into smaller steps, which are simpler to manage.

Prioritize based on the Purpose: Give the time and effort to each task in accordance with their importance and importance. It ensures that you are directing your energies into something that really matter to you.

Time Blocking Time Blocking: Allocate particular blocks of time to specific projects. This organized approach will help to ensure that you are making steady progress towards your objectives.

Infusing your life with clear objectives with prioritization and wisdom as well as the personal task order We can use our swords against the beast of procrastination. When we are on a path of intention that we take us from mindless drifting into a focused goal. Each time we step towards living a life that is formed by our decisions and guided by the goals we have set for ourselves. We must move forward and create an avenue that takes to a break with procrastination and toward the joy of achievement and progress.

Effective Time Management StrategiesTime is like a river that continues to flow in unending waves taking with it life-changing moments. When it comes to personal growth, mastering the skill of managing your time is like becoming an expert sailor, who can navigate the waters of life with precision and accuracy. This chapter will will reveal an array of time management techniques that will enable us to defeat delay and gain the upper hand of success.

6.1 The Pomodoro Technique

Imagine your time as a sequence of short, focused bursts with each of them accelerating you towards success. This is the Pomodoro Technique, named after the shape of a tomato in the kitchen timer makes use of the power of intervals to boost productivity.

How It Works:

1. Set a timer to run for about 25 mins (one Pomodoro).

2. Do your work in complete focus until the alarm goes off.

3. Stop for 5 minutes and refresh.

4. After you've completed the four Pomodoros after which you can take a more extended time break, 15-30 mins.

The benefit of this technique is that it makes use of the brain's ability to maintain focus over an indefinite period. Breaks are scheduled to prevent fatigue and keep the mind fresh.

6.2 Time Blocking for Maximum Efficiency

Imagine your entire day like a picture with each piece of time as an opportunity of productiveness. The art of time blocking that requires scheduling certain times for various tasks.

How It Works:

1. Break your day up in blocks in time (e.g. 30 minutes to one hour).

2. Assignment of tasks for each block and ensure that they are aligned to your goals.

3. Follow the plan and then move to the next step after the block has ended.

Benefit: Time-blocking provides an orderly system, which stops work from leaking into other. It helps focus, and reduces stress and fatigue in the decision-making process.

6.3 Harnessing the Two-Minute Rule

Imagine crossing a river swiftly that takes only a little effort. "The two-minute rule" a philosophies which encourages you to tackle small jobs promptly, instead of putting the task aside.

How It Works:

1. If the task is accomplished in a matter of two hours or less then complete it immediately.

2. If your task takes more time, include it on the list of tasks to be completed.

The benefit is that this rule stops the accumulation of smaller jobs that could become too much. It's an effective way to combat delay's hold on simple jobs.

6.4 Beating the Planning Fallacy

Imagine a map promising an adventure faster than the reality allows. Planning is a mistake. Planning Fallacy is the tendency to overestimate the time it takes for completing a task.

How to Beat It:

1. Reflecting on past experiences: Consider similar projects you've worked on previously. Utilize these as benchmarks when the estimation of duration.

2. Buffer Time Remember to add extra time to estimates in order to accommodate unexpected problems or delays.

3. Break tasks into smaller pieces: Separate the tasks into small steps. The time estimate to complete each task will be more precise than guessing about the whole task.

Benefit: Getting over this Planning Fallacy prevents frustration caused from unrealistic time expectations. You can ensure that you are allocating enough time for tasks, thus reducing your desire to delay tasks.

Chapter 4: Overcoming Procrastination Through Self-Discipline

In the turbulent motion of the world, discipline can be seen as a pillar that is unwaveringly committed. It's the compass to guide us in the storms of disorientation and the light which illuminates the way to success. This chapter will set off in a journey into the world of self-control which is a place where the intent transforms into action and procrastination fades into the dust.

7.1 Building Self-Discipline Muscles

Think of self-discipline as a muscular muscle that becomes stronger each time you use it. The process of building self-discipline muscle involves establishing behaviors and routines that help build the habit of being consistent and resilient.

Start Small: Get started with tasks you can accomplish. It will help you build a solid foundation for achievement, and reinforces your faith that you are able to remain focused.

Develop routines: Consistency breeds discipline. Set up daily routines to help you stay focused and prevent the fatigue that comes with making decisions.

Training in Delayed Gratitude: train your brain to avoid instant pleasure in favor of longer-term benefits. It rewires the brain to be able to see the bigger overall picture.

Be comfortable: Moving away from your comfort zone builds the self-discipline muscles. Accept challenges as an opportunity to grow.

7.2 Strategies for Improving Focus

Imagine focusing as a magnifying glass, which helps focus your focus on the job that is in front of you. To improve focus, you must create the right environment and mental state which minimizes distractions.

Create a space that is free of distractions: Set up a space free of distractions, such as phones or social media. Your brain will be notified to focus on your working.

Single-tasking: Multitasking squanders your focus, which reduces the effectiveness of your task. Focus on single-tasking and directing your attention to a single task at one moment.

Learn to practice mindfulness: It trains your mind to stay focused. Be fully engaged in every task by immersing yourself into the moment.

Time Blocking: Set aside certain blocks of time to concentrated tasks. When you are in these blocks, block out interruptions, and fully focus on the task at hand.

7.3 Using Rewards and Punishments Effectively

Consider rewards and penalties as rudders to guide your boat of self-control. Making them work effectively requires creating an organization that promotes positive behaviors and reduces the need for the habit of procrastination.

The Power of Rewards The rewards act as motivators that reinforce desired behaviour. Recognize your achievements by rewarding yourself with a meaningful reward.

The Effects of Punishments They act as deterrents and discourages you from putting off work. Make sure you have consequences for failure to keep your promises.

Develop Accountability: Share your goals with a trusted friend or mentor who will keep your accountable. The accountability layer adds a new level of motivation.

Gamification: Turn tasks into a game. Give rewards or points to those who complete their tasks within the timeframe creating a sense satisfaction.

If we go further into the world of self-discipline and discipline, we uncover an abundance of power and determination. The development of self-discipline muscle, sharpening the focus of our minds, and implementing rewarding and punishing behaviors that are effective can enable individuals to be successful in being proactive. Every step helps us change our perspective on the clock and our work. We rewrite the tale of procrastination revising it to be more purposeful.

The road ahead is one of introspective choice and constant commitment which means that each choice brings towards a future filled with accomplishments and progress.

The Role of Accountability

Consider accountability as a helping hand that gently guides forward along the way toward advancement. As a symphony for individual development, the power of accountability blends into self-control, creating an uplifting tune that smothers the sound of delay. This chapter will explore the intricate web of accountability as a factor which transforms thoughts into tangible action.

8.1 Finding an Accountability Partner

A accountability partner will be a similar-minded partner to help you reach your goal. They offer support, encouragement as well as a gentle push in times of need. It is a partnership built on the trust of each other and a shared dedication.

shared goals: Meet people who share similar goals or who is working towards your own ambitions. This understanding of each other adds more depth to your partnership.

Regular Check-ins: Create an appointment for check-ins on a regular basis. These meetings are a time of celebration, reflection as well as a chance to recalibrate.

Transparency: Honest communication is the basis of effective accountability. Communicate your accomplishments, problems as well as setbacks with openness.

A sense of encouragement and support: An accountability partner provides a secure area to share your doubts and fears. They can provide support and encouragement and remind the potential of you.

8.2 Utilizing Technology for Accountability

In this digital age, accountability goes beyond physical presence, taking on the world of technology. Technology for accountability requires making use of tools, applications and platforms to can help you keep track of your goals.

Task Management Software: Apps such as Todoist, Trello, or Asana assist you in organizing assignments, assign deadlines and keep track of the progress.

Habit Tracking apps: These applications assist you in creating good habits through reminders as well as tracking your progress.

Virtual Check-ins: Virtual meeting videos, phone calls, or text messages that include an accountability partner can help create a sense of belonging and accountability.

Social media Accountability Groups Forums, online communities and social media group with specific objectives offer an online support system.

8.3 Public Accountability and Its Benefits

Imagine that your pledge is broadcast as an advertisement for everyone to be able to see. Public accountability is the act of the sharing of your plans and accomplishments with a greater audience using the influence to influence social media.

Motivation by Visibility: When you have goals that are visible You're more likely to follow through with them, in order in order to avoid embarrassment the failure.

External Motivation External Motivation: External praise, encouragement and encouragement from the people you know fuel the fire that drives you.

Instilling a sense of responsibility Share your objectives with others creates an obligation to keep your word.

The creation of a supportive community: Public accountability could lead to friendships with people of like mind who provide support and sharing their experiences.

As part of the larger story of getting rid of indecision, accountability is an ever-present companion to you to guide your way. It doesn't matter if it's an accountability companion and tools for technology or even the gaze of a supportive group and the power of accountability can transform your path into a collaborative project.

When we accept this power as we move further into the realm of continuous behavior, where every move is guided by the purpose of each step and strengthened by connections. The chapters in this book reveal the power of accountability, which can be a catalyst to transform and growth.

Managing Perfectionism

The tapestry of our individual development, perfectionist tends to appears as a guide figure and a constant storm. The pursuit of excellence is laudable However, when perfectionists become a shackle that keeps our attention glued to apathy and inaction, we must break the grip of it. This chapter we'll explore the maze of perfectionists, discovering how we can harness its potential while freeing ourselves from its gripping power.

9.1 The Paralysis of Perfectionism

Imagine a sculptor chipping away at a slab of marble, constantly improving the edges to achieve perfectness. Like the sculptor's chisel can be used to create beautiful lines, but it also has the ability to frighten us with the pursuit of perfection.

The fear of failure: People who are perfectionists frequently fear that their works will not live up to their high standards. The fear can cause procrastination since starting is an invitation for failing.

Continuous Editing: The search for perfection could cause endless cycles of refining and editing and putting off the completion of projects.

Reduced Productivity: Perfectionism takes attention and energy away from actions, resulting in lower performance.

Negative self-talk: Perfectionists are known to be their most scathing critics. They engage with negative self-talk which affects their self-confidence.

9.2 Embracing Progress Over Perfection

Imagine a painter spreading his brush across a canvas, blending the canvas with vibrant colors which reflect the imperfections of life and the beauty. The process of embracing progress over perfection is switching your focus from perfection towards meaningful growth.

Enjoy Imperfections: Instead looking at imperfections as failures, look at them as the strokes that create your work as unique and real.

Create realistic standards: strive to be the best, but realize the fact that perfection is not a simple objective. Create achievable standards that will are challenging but don't overwhelm you.

Value Learning: Take on tasks using a perspective of development and learning. Every effort, regardless of whether it's success or failure, adds to your growth.

Focus on completion over perfection: Try to accomplish tasks rather than trying to make them perfect. The satisfaction of completing tasks gives you a sense satisfaction and encourages you to keep going.

9.3 Strategies for Overcoming Perfectionist Tendencies

Imagine yourself on a boat navigating treacherous waterways, staying clear of the sharp rocks of perfection. In order to overcome perfectionist tendencies, it is necessary to adopt techniques that allow it to loosen and allow you to act.

Create Time Limits: Dedicate the appropriate period of time to each project. After the allotted time has expired you can move on regardless of whether your task is completed.

Keep your eyes on the big Picture Keep in mind the ultimate objective. What is the significance of this project to the larger scope of things?

Break down tasks into smaller pieces Perfectionist tends to thrive when projects seem to be daunting. By breaking them down into manageable, smaller steps eases pressure.

Be kind to yourself: treat yourself with compassion and kindness. Be aware that imperfections and mistakes are normal parts of your journey.

Chapter 5: Cultivating Motivation And Inspiration

Within the world of personal growth Motivation and inspiration can be the seedlings that bloom into extraordinary successes. They're the fuel which propels us forward. They are the wind that fills our sails, and the flame that sparks the passions of our hearts. This chapter will begin on a path to nurture the rich soil of our dreams, nourishing the foundations of intrinsic and external motivations, while creating the tapestry of our imagination and vision.

10.1 Identifying Intrinsic and Extrinsic Motivators

Think of motivation as a dual-fuel engine driven by inner desires as well as external reward. Understanding intrinsic as well as extrinsic motivations requires understanding the forces that drive you to act.

Instinct motivation: They are inner motivations that stem from your personal beliefs and desires. They create a sense satisfaction and purpose.

Extrinsic Motivations: These are external rewards like the recognition of money, recognition or even praise. Although they are powerful however, depending solely on them may result in a weak and sluggish motivation.

Balance between extrinsic and intrinsic motivation can create a strong synergy. Instinctual motivators keep you going through your journey. Extrinsic reward systems provide milestones for celebration.

10.2 Tapping Into Your Passion

Imagine your passion as a flame which is bright and shining, lighting even the darkest parts of your life. Engaging in your passion requires using your energy to achieve the thing that sets your heart on fire.

Review your Interests: Think about the activities that bring you joy and lively. They can help you find your interests.

Be Connected to Your Values It is common for passion to arise from alignment to your fundamental values. If your actions are reflective of your values most important to you Passion ignites.

Be curious: Discover new places and let your the curiosity guide you. It can be a result of excitement at discovering new things.

The commitment to challenge yourself Passion does not exempt you from failure However, it does infuse your work with a unwavering dedication.

10.3 Creating a Vision Board for Long-Term Motivation

Visualize your goals as pieces of a puzzle that are waiting to be put together into an amazing image. Making a vision board is creating a visual representation of your dreams and goals.

Collect Materials: Gather images of quotes, items, and images that align with your vision.

This can be cut out from magazines, printed or designed digitally.

Visualize Your Dreams: Place the materials you have on a table that represents your goals. It is a tangible way to keep your objectives in the forefront.

Daily Affirmation: Take just an hour or so every day looking over your dream board. Imagine your accomplishment and feel the feelings associated with reaching the goals you set.

Use Inspiration to inspire you Vision boards serve as a source of inspiration when you are struggling or experiencing exhaustion.

When we explore the complex environments of motivation and inspiration We discover the core of our goals. In balancing intrinsic and external motivators inflaming our passions creating visual reminders, and putting them into words propel us towards a consistent path. The chapter we're in will create the story of our lives that is driven by passion and lit by enthusiasm. Each step of the way the journey is infused with significance and remind us that the road towards overcoming indecision is made by bright colors of inspiration.

Overcoming Procrastination Through Mindfulness

Procrastination is a term that is a source of frustration as well as the familiarity. Everyone has been there: postponing tasks, delay assignments, only to be stuck in a vicious cycle of inefficiency. In the preceding chapters, we've examined the various ways to recognize and overcome the habit of procrastination. This chapter, we'll shift our focus to the potential of mindfulness as a technique which can change the way we approach tasks as well as manage our emotions and eventually free us from the grip of procrastination.

11.1 Practicing Mindfulness Meditation

In a culture that emphasizes multitasking and continual activities, the idea of mindfulness provides a new view. The practice of mindfulness is to cultivate a greater awareness of what is happening in the moment with no judgment. Through consistent mindfulness practice you can stop the whirring of the mind and refocus our focus on the present and the present. We'll explore ways this practice is a great instrument in fighting the urge to delay.

Mindful Breathing: Your Anchor to the Present

Start by locating a comfy and tranquil spot. Relax your eyes, and pay the focus of your breath. Experience the sensations of every breath and exhale. The breath is an anchor, a place of concentration that you are able to be sure to return to whenever your mind wanders. Pay attention to the rising and falling of your chest and the pattern of your breathing. If thoughts arise The things you must accomplish, thoughts regarding the future, acknowledge the thoughts with no judgement, and slowly return your focus to the breath.

The Body scan: Tuning In to your physical sensations

A different method of meditation with mindfulness is to do a body scan. Begin at the upper part of your head, as you gradually work your way towards your body. Be aware of any areas that are prone to tension, pain, or perhaps ease. It isn't the intention to alter anything however, it is to simply observe. Most often, procrastination is caused by anxiety and stress. Body scans help to make you more sensitive to the feelings, which allows you to deal with them effective.

Mindful Observation: Engaging Your Senses

When you're going around your daily routine, spend a few minutes with your mind. Select an object that might be a pen as well as a blossom or even a basic raisins. Take a close look as if looking at it for the very first second time. Pay attention to the colors, textures and the specifics. Use your other senses to ponder - What is it odor and sound like? Or experience as? The practice does not just bring your attention to the present but also prepares your mind to concentrate in the present moment.

11.2 Mindful Approaches to Task Engagement

Procrastination can be triggered by absence of interest and an overwhelming feeling. A shift in mindset can alter the way you handle the tasks you have to complete, making them more achievable and fun. Explore some of the mindful strategies for task involvement that could assist you to break free of the grasp of the habit of procrastination.

Single-Tasking: Embracing the Power of One

In an age that demands multi-tasking the idea of focusing on just one thing may seem unnatural. Yet, mindfulness shows the importance of paying total focus to just one task at a given time is extremely satisfying.

While you do something avoid the temptation to look at your phone, reply to emails or change between different tabs. Instead, be fully immersed into the work. Pay attention to the small details, the subtleties, and the progress that you're taking.

Setting Mindful Intentions: Creating Clarity

Before beginning a task make a point to establish a clear intention. What goals do you want to accomplish? What is the best way to tackle this challenge? A clear intention can bring clarity on your actions, and can help to ensure that they are aligned to your objectives. If, for instance, you're engaged in a difficult project the goal might be to focus on growing and growing rather than perfectionism.

Finding Flow: The Dance of Effort and Ease

The notion of "flow" is when you're totally engaged in a task that you lose the track of your time and worries. The practice of mindfulness can allow you to tap into this state more frequently. When you are working at a job take note of your rhythm, the balance between ease and effort. Be aware of when you begin to be overwhelmed or stressed as you gently bring your attention on the task at hand. Be aware of your mental situation can stop procrastination from getting in the way.

11.3 Enhancing Emotional Regulation

The process of putting off work is usually entwined with the emotions we feel. Sometimes, we put off tasks due to the fact that they cause emotions of anxiety, stress or even bored. Mindfulness provides us with the tools to manage these feelings and help us beat the desire to delay tasks.

Embracing Uncomfortable Emotions: The R.A.I.N. Technique

The R.A.I.N. technique is a method of mindfulness that assists you in dealing with emotional issues in a loving method.

Start by acknowledging the emotion you're feeling. Are you feeling anger, fear or a different emotion? When you acknowledge the emotion it allows you to manage it.

Let the emotion to feel and not try to dispel it. This is the process of letting the resistance that you have to the emotion, and then being able to feel the emotion completely.

Explore: Carefully explore the physical sensations linked to emotions. Do you feel tension in your chest, or an abdominal knot? Explore these symptoms with curiosity.

Nurture: Lastly give yourself a hug and a little love. Consider what you'd tell a friend suffering from the same emotions. Give yourself that same kind of kindness.

Cultivating a Growth Mindset: From Failure to Learning

A shift in your mindset can alter your perception of setsbacks and mistakes. Instead of looking at these as a reason to quit or delay, view these challenges with a mindset of growth. Mindfulness shows us that each event, no matter how difficult can be used to grow and learn. If you experience the pitfalls of life, you should consider a moment of reflection about the lessons it teaches. A shift in perspective can lessen the impact on your emotions of failure, and help you to remain committed to the goals you have set.

Celebrating Small Wins: Gratitude and Positivity

The practice of mindfulness can also help you cultivate positive and gratitude. Most often, the cause of procrastination stems from negative thinking or the focus on things that are happening. You can combat this by constantly appreciating and celebrating little successes. Have you completed a project faster than anticipated? Have you met a hurdle? Make a point to appreciate these triumphs, and let them feed your drive to move ahead.

In the field of mindfulness it is clear that mindfulness has a profound effect on the way we can overcome the habit of procrastination. When we practice mindfulness meditation using mindful strategies for tasks, and strengthening our ability to regulate emotions We are equipped with the tools to help us break free from the chains of procrastination.

By focusing on mindfulness, we realize that being present in the moment is the place where we have power and the ability to act, achieve improvements, and eventually define our own pathways toward the success we desire.

How to Build Habits to be SuccessfulAs our quest to overcome procrastination goes on as we come to an essential point in the science and art of creating habits that will lead to successful outcomes. Habits are invisible threads that influence the way we act, behave as well as the outcomes we achieve. This chapter will explore the impact that habits have in our capacity to get rid of the habit of procrastination, and to take steady steps towards our desired goals.

12.1 The Science of Habit Formation

Habits are brain's method to save energy. They help us automate repetitive tasks and free the brain space to make higher-level decision-making. Knowing the science behind how habits form helps us harness the natural processes to create positive changes.

The Habit Loop: Cue, Routine, Reward

The underlying principle of each routine is a basic loop that includes cue routine, cue and reward. Cues trigger an action, and the pattern will lead to the behaviour, and the reward enlarges the pattern. Consider that you are accustomed to checking your the social networks when bored (cue). Then you go over your newsfeed (routine) then you notice that the constant stream of posts and updates gives you an impression of excitement and connections (reward). The understanding of this loop enables us to analyze our current habits and create fresh ones.

Neuroplasticity: Rewiring the Brain for Change

The brain's capacity to change the wiring of itself, also known as neuroplasticity, is an important factor in the formation of habit. When we repeat an action and the neural pathways that are associated with the behavior get stronger. As time passes, this process will make the action more natural and simple. When we intentionally create new habits, it is possible to alter our brains so that they are in alignment with the actions we want to take.

The 21/90 Rule: Forming Lasting Habits

Although there is no magic amount of time it takes to establish a habit, the rule of 21/90 is a useful guidance. A commitment to a particular behavior over a period of 21 days could build the foundation. However, adhering to it for a period of 90 days establishes the habit as an ongoing one. It is crucial to be consistent - each when you do the same thing it reinforces neural pathways and make your habit stronger and more permanent.

12.2 Keystone Habits and Their Impact

Keystone behaviors are similar to the fundamentals of the foundation. they create ripple effects that influences other aspects of our life. If we can identify and cultivate the keystone habits, we are able to create positive changes that go over the beginning of our habit.

Exercise: A Keystone Habit for Well-Being

Imagine the possibility of introducing a regular workout regimen into your daily routine. It is a key habit that is not just beneficial for the physical condition of your body but also results in improved mental wellbeing. While you are engaged with physical exercise there is a release of endorphins, the "feel-good" chemicals. Your newfound enthusiasm and energy may spill out to other areas of your life, empowering people to complete tasks which you'd otherwise put off about.

Mindful Eating: A Ripple Effect on Productivity

Another keystone activity that can be a powerful one is eating mindfully. If you take your time and take time to enjoy your meals and eat mindfully, you develop mindfulness -- which carries onto your work chores. By focusing and staying present your chances are less to be distracted and cause yourself to procrastinate. In addition, eating mindfully often will result in better level of energy, which can boost your productivity overall.

Journaling: Unleashing Creativity and Clarity

Journaling as a habit is an incredibly versatile practice that has a wide range of benefits. While you pen on paper, you let loose your creative side and become more clear about your feelings and thoughts. The practice leads to increased decision-making ability, decreased stress and an enhanced feeling of self-awareness. A calm mind is less prone to the grip of procrastination.

12.3 Habit Stacking for Consistency

Consistency is at the core of habits. Habit stacking is an approach which uses existing patterns to help you develop new ones. In leveraging the behavior that you are already performing regularly it is possible to introduce fresh habits without difficulty to your daily routine.

Identifying Anchor Habits: Your Starting Point

Start by identifying your anchoring practices - habits that are regular parts of your daily routine. They could be that is as basic as cleaning your teeth or drinking the morning cup of coffee or showering. These routines serve as triggers to encourage new behavior.

Pairing New Habits: Creating a Chain Reaction

After you've found an routine that you are accustomed to, combine it with a brand new one you're looking to establish. As an example, if you regularly drink a cup of tea at the end of your afternoon, it could be a good idea to pair it with a 10 minute stretch routine. As time passes, the ritual of sipping tea will become the trigger for you to start the stretching routine. This effect of chaining makes your new habits more likely to be a habit.

Celebrating Small Wins: Reinforcing the Loop

Be sure to remember that each moment you are successful in the new routine, you should celebrate the achievement. It's small reward, which helps to reinforce the loop of habit. Each time you repeat it this behavior gets more effortless, and procrastination is finding it difficult to keep from slipping in.

In the process of building habit it is possible to harness the power of habit-building to create a strong power for transformation. With a thorough understanding of the concept of how habits form as well as the cultivation of keystone habit patterns, and the application of habit stacking creating a system that pushes our progress.

Chapter 6: Boosting Creativity And Innovation

The labyrinth of personal development, in which your quest for efficiency is interspersed with personal discovery, lies a place that is often filled with the fire of imagination. In this section we will explore the synergistic connection between innovation, creativity and fighting procrastination. While we travel together we'll show you how to unleash the unbridled power of your imagination to overcome the procrastination which once put you off.

13.1 Procrastination's Effects on Creativity

The two may appear as if they are not related, but within the complex tapestry of our human brains the two are interwoven threads. In the first place it appears that procrastination is the enemy of productivity hindering creativity, and leaving us trapped in the tangle of lack of action. But the reality is far more nuanced.

The Struggle Between Immediate Gratification and Creative Exploration

Procrastination can be triggered by an urge to get immediate satisfaction such as the dopamine rush from social media, or the convenience of working on a routine task. It can be difficult to see the less subtle, unpredictability and incredibly rewarding road of exploration. When you put off creative endeavors you fall into a the routine of your life which makes it more difficult to take on the unfamiliar landscape of creativity.

The Perfectionism Paradox

The concept of perfectionism, which is a cousin of procrastination, may inhibit the creativity. A fear of making an item that is flawless could lead to inertia - you put off starting due to the fact that your final product may not match your expectations. Insufficiency can take enjoyment out of your creative process and lead to delay.

13.2 Fostering a Creative Mindset

Creativity is the mental state and a way of thinking that turns everyday things into something remarkable. To overcome the habit of procrastination, you must developing a mindset of creativity which helps you act. Learn how you can change your mindset to bring an increase in creativity to your daily life.

Embrace Imperfection: The Beauty of Flaws

One of the most liberating ways towards a more creative mind is accepting the imperfections. Recognize that the process of creativity is messy, characterized by the process of trial and error. Instead of avoiding the failures, consider them steps towards growth. When you let off the desire for perfection, you encourage interest and curiosity.

Cultivate Curiosity: Fuel for Creativity

The source of curiosity is that inspires creativity. Begin tasks with a sense of curiosity, engaging in conversation and looking for fresh perspectives. If curiosity is your driving source of light, you lose procrastination's grasp - instead, you're motivated by curiosity and not the pressure of accomplishment.

Embody Mindfulness: Engage the Senses

Mindfulness isn't only a method to help you overcome the urge to procrastinate; it's an avenue to imagination. Involving your senses and putting you completely in the time creates a more receptive mindset. When you look at the world surrounding you - the colours and textures, the sounds you create a deep supply of ideas.

13.3 Creative Techniques to Break Procrastination

Creativity goes beyond an idea - it's an array of strategies to spark your creativity and spur you to take the action. We'll explore some innovative techniques that will assist you to escape the grip of putting off work.

Divergent Thinking: Exploring Many Avenues

Divergent thinking is an approach that allows you to investigate many possibilities. If you are faced with a problem to solve, think about a broad range of thoughts without judging. Quality, not quantity will be the primary focus. This method avoids self-censorship often associated with the habit of procrastination. It gives an array of possibilities to pick from.

Mind Mapping: Organising ideas visually

Mind maps are a graphic tool that lets you arrange your thoughts and ideas. Beginning with a basic idea and then expand with other related concepts. As you build your mind's map it will become clearer about your task and make it much easier to make decisions. Mind mapping is a way to engage both brains encouraging holistic thinking and creative thinking.

The 20-Second Rule: Lowering Activation Energy

The 20-second rule is an easy technique to decrease the energy needed to initiate a project. Make it easier for people to enter by making the first tasks as straightforward as is possible. If, for instance, you are planning to write, you should keep your pen and notebook at a distance of 20 seconds. If you can reduce the friction involved in getting started, you'll be possible to stop procrastinating.

In the journey of encouraging the ability to think creatively and overcome procrastination we create a web of potential. When you cultivate a mindset of creativity accepting imperfection and employing innovative techniques to create a safe haven in which procrastination is able to flourish. With creativity, you will discover the power of imagination and action together, guiding you towards the realm of creativity and achievement.

Overcoming Procrastination in Decision Making

In the midst of our personal growth, the process of making a decision is a crucial step between the goals we have in mind as well as the steps we choose to take. In many cases, procrastination casts shadows over this critical junction that leaves us in a state of panic due to fears of making poor decisions. The chapter we're in will set off on a mission to show the pathway to self-assured decision-making and free us from the shackles of anxiety and uncertainty.

14.1 The Fear of Making Wrong Decisions

Fear of making a mistake in choices is an all-encompassing factor that can lead us into delay. We put off decisions, hoping that it will be a time of clarity and confidence. This delay can cause us to be stuck in an unproductive state which can impede growth and progress.

The Paralysis of Analysis: When Overthinking Takes Over

Overthinking is an opportune response to fear of making incorrect decisions. It is a habit of analyzing every possibility and try to find the assurance that we will make the right decision. In reality, the exhaustive process could lead to decision fatigue. The stress of analyzing every aspect becomes too much, leading us to put off making a decision entirely.

Regret and Avoidance: The Dance of Uncertainty

The fear of regret can be big in the process of making decisions. The fear is of looking back, to realize that we chose the wrong decision. It can lead us to eschew making a decision entirely - an apparently safe option that can actually encourage the cycle of procrastination. If we can frame regret as a chance to learn and rethinking the way we view decisions.

14.2 Strategies for Confident Decision Making

The ability to make informed decisions is a capability that can be developed by committing to regular practices and mental changes. If you adopt these methods to make decisions, you will be able to navigate the maze of decisions in a clear and confident manner.

Clarify Your Values: Your Inner Compass

Start by defining your core values, the guidelines that guide your daily course. When your choices are in line with your ideals and beliefs, they are more consistent and genuine. If you can identify what really matters for you, you can create a solid foundations on that you can base your decisions.

Set Boundaries on Information Seeking: The Quest for Certainty

In this age of information, the constant search for certainty could result in a continuous loop of trying to find additional data. Instead of becoming a squid in an endless sea of data, put guidelines for your research. Set a deadline for your study, and once the time has passed be sure to take a your decision using the data that you've got.

Practice Decisiveness: From Small to Large Choices

The muscle of decision-making is able to be developed by practicing. Make small-scale decisions like which clothes to wear, and food choices - slowly moving towards more complex options. Every choice you make will strengthen the confidence you have in your own judgement and continue to continue to move forward in confidence.

14.3 Making Learning Lessons from Failure With No Regret

A journey to make a confident choice taking isn't without obstacles and detours. Failures and mistakes are constant partners, but they do not have to not remain a constant obstacle. If you are able to embrace a more growth-oriented approach it is possible to gain knowledge from the mistakes you made and avoid remorse.

Cultivate a Growth Mindset: From Failure to Learning

The growth mindset changes the focus of your mind from failing to growing. Instead of seeing a choice made in error as proof to your shortcomings, look at the situation as an opportunity to development. What can you learn from this experience? How do you use these insights to make the future?

Practice Reflection: Unpacking the Lessons

Once you've made your decision then take some time to think about your decision. Which of the decisions worked? What failed? What would you have done differently the next time? Reflection can transform the mistakes you made into learning points that will lead you to better informed decisions in the near future.

The Embrace Course Correction by Pivoting with The Purpose

If your decision isn't able to produce the outcome you want, take advantage of the possibility of direction adjustment. Instead of reliving regret, pivot to the desired outcome.

Change your approach, change the way you approach it, then go forward using a fresh perspective. It is this ability to adjust that is an attribute of a the most resilient individuals.

In the process of making decisions We realize that delay is often disguised as being cautious. When we overcome fears of making erroneous choices, implementing strategies to make confidence-based choices, and gaining knowledge from mistakes without regret, we are able to confidently move towards the intersection of opportunities. Through the dance of the two and action, we affirm our position in determining our own destiny.

Chapter 7: Navigating Procrastination In The Digital Age

The world of personal growth Digital technology offers endless opportunities, as well as unimaginable difficulties. Technology has led to connectivity, information and a greater degree of convenience, it's created different forms of procrastination. In this article we will explore the interplay between technology and procrastination and discover strategies for creating a an aesthetically pleasing digital presence which can inspire actions.

15.1 The Impact of Technology on Procrastination

In a time that a plethora of information resides within our fingers, the effect that technology has on procrastination is not to be overlooked. The enticement of social media as well as the continual flow of notifications, as well as the endless rabbit holes that exist in internet-based content could create ideal environment in which procrastination can flourish.

The Dopamine Loop: Pleasure and Distraction

The technology, specifically social media platforms trigger the reward system in our brains and releases dopamine after each tweet, comment or share. The dopamine cycle can turn addicted, pulling users away from their work and into endless scrolling. In the instant, instant pleasure offered by technology could stifle our attention, which makes difficult to do long-lasting, productive work.

The Myth of Multitasking: Divided Attention

Technology is often used to create the illusion of multitasking. It is juggling many things at once. Yet, studies have shown that the concept of multitasking is actually not a reality. Brains are not built to be able to handle multiple tasks simultaneously, resulting in lower productivity, and an increased probability of procrastination.

15.2 Digital Detox and Its Benefits

With the constant whirlwind of technology it is the idea to detox digitally comes into play as a source of calm. Digital detox is the deliberate disconnection from electronic gadgets and applications for a predetermined time. This method can offer a wide range of advantages that go beyond the short-term removal of technology.

Restoring Mental Clarity: A Breather for the Mind

Continuous exposure to digital stimulation could overwhelm your mind and result in decisions fatigue. Digital detox can provide the chance to breathe - an opportunity for your brain to refocus, reset and recharge. The renewed focus can assist people approach their work from an enlightened perspective and reduce the urge to put off tasks.

Reclaiming Time: Redirecting Energy

It is no wonder that the hours you spend browsing through social media sites or browsing the internet can accumulate quickly. Digital detox can allow users to take back their time, and channel your attention towards more fulfilling activities. If you take part in activities that are in line with your dreams and interests, putting off work finds it difficult to establish its claims.

Cultivating Mindfulness: An Offline Experience

Digital detoxes encourage a returning to the present. In the absence of constant alerts, you are able to participate actively regardless of whether you're going for a walk, reading a book an outing, or simply enjoying time with family members. Being present can translate to increased focus, making it simpler to withstand the lure of putting off tasks.

15.3 Establishing Healthy Online Boundaries

While technology is an integral part of modern life, establishing healthy boundaries can help you navigate the digital realm without succumbing to its procrastination-inducing traps.

Designated Tech-Free Zones: Sacred Spaces

Set up designated zones for technology-free areas within your workspace or at home. They act as safe zones away from all the digital noise that allow you to concentrate in a relaxed, relaxing and connected in a safe and peaceful environment. Consider, for instance, establishing your bedroom to be a non-tech space to encourage restful sleep and lessen the urge to spend your evening scrolling.

Scheduled Digital Engagement: Mindful Consumption

Instead of constantly connected to the devices you use Schedule specific times to engage in engaging with the internet. Set aside certain times during the day for checking messages, social networks and various other internet-related activities. When you set limits allow you to take control of your online activities and decrease the chance of falling into the trap of procrastination.

Notification Management: Curating Distractions

Make sure you are aware of notifications. Block unnecessary notifications and other notifications that interfere with your concentration. This straightforward step can reduce interruptions and allows you to concentrate on your work with no interruptions from notifications and pings.

In the current technological age, our balance between productivity and technology is dependent on the ability of us to establish the boundaries we want to set. Through understanding the effects technological advancements on procrastination taking advantage of the benefits of detoxing from digital clutter and setting guidelines for our online presence We can build a virtual presence that is an opportunity for growth, instead of a barrier for advancement. As we dance between the digital and the physical and the real, we can regain our power and begin to step into the world filled with purposeful actions.

Overcoming Procrastination in Academics and Work

In the busy world of academia and work and work, procrastination could cast a shadow over our goals. If it's studying for tests as well as meeting deadlines or working towards continuous improvement and improvement, procrastination can have the remarkable capability of stalling the progress we make. This chapter will go in a quest to discover the intricate ways to defeat procrastination within the world of academics and at work. We will arm our minds with the most effective methods for embracing productivity and growing.

16.1 Effective Study and Work Techniques

The efficiency of academics and at work is based on efficient study techniques and methods of work. If you can master these strategies and techniques, you will be able to transform the process of production and studying into an efficient procedure that reduces the impact of the habit of putting off work.

The Pomodoro Technique: Time as a Friend

The Pomodoro Technique is a method of managing time which breaks down tasks into concentrated periods of time, typically approximately 25 minutes in length, then with a break of a few minutes. This method capitalizes on your brain's ability to stay focused in a short amount of period of time. If you can break down tasks into small chunks it makes them less daunting and less likely to delay.

Chunking: Organizing for Clarity

Chunking is the process of breaking large task into smaller, manageable pieces. The brain's tendency to process information into smaller chunks. Each time you take on a chunk and you feel a sense of achievement, which motivates your to continue moving ahead.

Spaced Repetition: Efficient Learning

Spaced repetition is an investigation method that requires revisiting data in a series of intervals that increase in the course of time. This technique leverages the space effect. Information is more easily retained if reviewed with intervals of space. This method will help it improves your learning which reduces the need to cram last minute.

16.2 Beating Deadlines and Avoiding Last-Minute Rush

Deadlines, which loom like sentinels have the ability to create a climate of the urge to delay. But, by implementing methods that address deadlines in a proactive manner and avoid rushes of the last minute you can reduce the enticement of procrastination.

Time Blocking: A Proactive Approach

Time blocking is the process of scheduling certain times for various activities. If you allocate times for working break, study and breaks, you can create the framework for a routine which reduces chances of putting off work. If you follow your timetable, the stress of deadlines looming disappears.

Reverse Engineering: Beginning with the end in mind

Reverse engineering involves beginning by defining the goal, then moving backwards in order to make an outline. When you break tasks down into small, manageable steps, you build an outline that will guide the way to get there. This method eliminates the stress that can cause delay.

Accountability Partners: Shared Commitment

A partner who is accountable can provide a significant solution to the habit of procrastination. If you can share your objectives and timeframes with someone else you build a sense accountability. Being aware that somebody is trusting you will give the drive needed to stay in the right direction and to meet deadlines.

16.3 Strategies for Continuous Learning and Improvement

Within the world of academics as well as work, the path does not end when you finish a task and completing deadlines. Continuous learning and development are the foundation of progress. If you implement strategies to encourage continual development, you will develop a mental attitude that is more than just delay.

Kaizen: The Power of Small Steps

Kaizen which is the Japanese concept, is based on the concept of continual growth through incremental, small measures. Focusing on incremental, steady improvements you can create the impression of growth and momentum. This helps to reduce the need to delay growth-related activities.

Feedback Loops: Embracing Constructive Input

Feedback loops require seeking and accepting constructive feedback for improvement of your skills and improve your performance. When you seek out feedback, you're opening your mind to opportunities for growth and eliminate the fear of failing. This shift in perspective reduces the urge to delay work because due to fear of failure.

Celebrating Wins: Reinforcing Positive Habits

Be proud of your accomplishments, little and big. When you celebrate your achievements and achievements, you encourage positive attitudes and behavior. Positive reinforcement can encourage you to take steps and persist even when you are tempted to delay.

While we weave the intricate multi-layered world of study and work it becomes apparent that procrastination is usually disguised as a distraction from the path of progress.

Through embracing efficient methods of study and working by proactively meeting deadlines and cultivating a culture of continual learning, we can create an approach that is rooted in purpose and success. Through the dance of the two We choose the actions which will lead to growth and achievement.

Building Resilience against Procrastination In the thicket of our personal growth, resilience is seen as a symbol of resilience when faced with adversity. In the battle against procrastination, building a resilient mindset isn't merely a way to do it It's an integral part to live your living. This chapter will dive in to the process of protecting yourself from the ravages of procrastination. We will also discuss how to overcome relapses and defeat, and arming yourself with an arsenal of anti-procrastination tools which can stand up to the test of the passage of time.

17.1 Understanding Procrastination Relapses

Relapses in procrastination are a normal element of getting free. Instead of looking at these mistakes as failures they can be seen as an opportunity to gain knowledge and improve.

The Cyclical Nature of Progress

The pace of progress is not always linear. Like the seasons, which alter, so does the relationship you have to delay. You must realize that a relapse won't undo your progress. It's more of a temporary divergence from the path of change.

Triggers and Patterns

Finding triggers that cause the relapse of procrastination is a crucial measure to build resilient. The triggers could be internal (emotions and ideas) and external (environments or conditions,). Understanding patterns will help to avoid possible pitfalls.

17.2 The Return of Procrastination Episodes

Recovering from the procrastination lapses involves reflection, self-compassion, as well as actionable actions. The goal is to learn from the experiences without letting it determine you.

Practice Self-Compassion: Be Your Own Ally

Instead of criticizing yourself for procrastinating instead, cultivate self-compassion. Take care of yourself the way you would an intimate friend who stumbles. Accept the fall and acknowledge the strength you have to get to the top.

Reflect and Learn: The Power of Introspection

Pause to think about the time you spent procrastinating. What was the trigger? What thoughts or emotions played a role? What might you have avoided? The process of reflection provides useful insights which can help you plan your next decisions.

Set Small Goals: Regaining Momentum

Following a time of procrastination Set small, achievable objectives. This will help you get back a sensation of motivation and achievement. Once you have achieved the goals you set, you build confidence and drive.

17.3 Strengthening Your Anti-Procrastination Arsenal

Resilience against procrastination requires having a solid arsenal of strategies and tools. The tools you have are your arsenal to fight the grip of procrastination.

Positive Affirmations: Rewriting Self-Talk

Make positive affirmations that combat the self-deflection that typically is associated with delay. Repetition these affirmations often to shift your thinking and improve your self-esteem.

Visual Reminders: Reinforcing Intentions

Utilize visual reminders to keep track of your objectives and plans. It could be a vision board, a notepad at your desk, or a screensaver for your device. They help keep you focused on the direction you want to go and can help prevent the urge to delay.

Reward Systems: Celebrating Progress

Establish a system for rewards to reward you. If you complete goals or reach goals, reward yourself by doing an enjoyable reward. The rewards can make positive associations when you take actions and help to counter the temptation to delay.

Support System: Allies in Resilience

Connect with supportive people - your parents, relatives, or friends and others who can relate to your issues and encourage your spirits. Supporting your network gives the strength you need during tough times, and helps you remember that you're not on your own in the journey.

Mindfulness and Stress Management: Balancing Emotions

The practice of mindfulness and stress management methods can assist you in navigating the psychological terrain that frequently causes procrastination. If you're grounded and manage your stress levels, you'll be better prepared to confront challenges and not resort to avoidance.

In the course towards building resilience to resist procrastination, it becomes clear that setbacks aren't barriers, but rather steps to take. When we understand relapses and bounce back using self-compassion as well as accumulating an effective anti-procrastination strategy, we can strengthen our determination to persevere to pursue our objectives. Through the dance of failures and growth We emerge as strong warriors who see the challenges we face as an opportunity to grow.

Chapter 8: Creating An Environment For Productivity

When it comes to personal development, the setting within which we work is a significant motivator or an enormous obstacle to our efforts. In the battle against the urge to delay, creating the right environment to boost efficiency is an essential approach. In this section we explore the intricate details of how the physical environment influences our behaviors, look into how to organize workspaces to maximize efficiency, and explore the power of the environment to prompt active behavior.

18.1 The Impact of Physical Spaces on Procrastination

The environments we live in influence the way we think and behave. The environment we design could either encourage focused actions or, in a way, encourage delay.

The Psychology of Spaces: Influencing Behavior

Our environment plays an important role in influencing our thinking behavior, feelings, and emotions. An unorganized, messy space could trigger feelings of overwhelming and disorientation, which makes it more likely to fall prey to a tendency to delay. However, a tidy and well-organized space will bring focus and clarity which can lead to greater productive work.

Physical Triggers: Prompts for Action

Spaces in the physical can serve as triggers to perform certain actions. As an example, the simple posture of your desk could signal to your brain you're ready to get started. Utilizing these triggers it is possible to make seamless shift from intent into action, decreasing the chance of procrastination.

18.2 Organizing Your Workspace for Optimal Efficiency

An organized workspace isn't simply a neat collection of things It's an organized design that optimizes effectiveness and reduces distractions. If you can optimize your workspace, you'll set the conditions for a smooth and efficient work experience.

Decluttering: Clearing Mental Noise

Get started by cleaning out your workspace. Eliminate items that do not contribute directly to your current tasks. The clutter creates mental distraction which can cause delay. Clean slates allow for greater focus and more effective making decisions.

Functional Design: Layout for Flow

Think about what layout you want for your work space. Sort items according to their frequency of use as well as importance. Place frequently used tools in reach, eliminating any need for continuous interruptions and search. The strategic arrangement promotes an easy workflow while reducing the possibility of having to switch tasks.

Personalization: Infusing Inspiration

Make your work space a place to be filled with things which inspire your. It doesn't matter if it's a motivating statement, a visual board or art which resonates with your objectives Personal touches like these could inspire motivation and enthusiasm to make procrastination seem like a non-issue. option.

18.3 Using Environmental Cues to Trigger Action

The environmental cues provide subtle cues that trigger certain actions. Through strategically placing signals throughout your surroundings, you are able to influence yourself to take action.

Task-Specific Zones: Designating Purpose

Designate task-specific zones in the environment. Designate zones for focus as well as relaxation and breaks. If you are in these zones you'll receive brain signals concerning the task in mind which reduces the possibility of distractedness or procrastination.

Color Psychology: Harnessing Visual Stimuli

Colors influence our mood as well as our behavior. Utilize color in a strategic way within your surroundings to increase concentration and drive. Blue, for instance can be associated with peace and concentration. Red is a great way to boost energy and focus to the smallest of details.

Digital Environment: Taming Digital Distractions

Expand your attention from the your surroundings to the realm of digital. Sort your files in digital format clean your desktop and make use of website blocking software to reduce the online distractions. Through optimizing your digital workspace and creating the perfect environment to meet your goals for productivity.

While we explore the world of work, we see that the environment we live in is the canvas on where our plans are realized. Through recognizing the influence of the physical space, arranging spaces to maximize efficiency using environmental cues to guide us to create an environment that maximizes our capabilities and removes barriers to inefficiency. Through the interplay between our environments and activities We emerge as the architects of an environment that pushes us towards the goal of achieving our goals.

Sustaining Long-Term Procrastination Breakthroughs

While we traverse the valley of personal growth and overcoming the habit of procrastination is an incredible achievement. But, it isn't finished with just one triumph. To sustain long-term growth, you must commit to vigilance and a plan in order to stop a decline. In this chapter, we will dive into the practice of celebrating accomplishments and milestones, look at ways to prevent Relapses, and explore the fundamentals of an active and proactive way of life.

19.1 Celebrating Milestones and Achievements

The joy of celebrating milestones and accomplishments doesn't only serve to give yourself a pat on the for a job well done. It's an essential aspect of keeping momentum going and keep you motivated in the fight to beat the urge to delay.

Reflect and Appreciate: A Pause for Gratitude

Spend some time reflecting on the journey you've taken and be grateful for the way you've progressed. Consider the accomplishments that you've made. It could be finishing a project without delay or avoiding your regular routine. The practice of being grateful boosts the feeling of achievement and increases your determination to carry on.

Rewarding Yourself: Acknowledging Effort

Recognize yourself for the achievements you've made. The rewards you receive don't have to be expensive They could be as easy like treating yourself to an indulgence at a restaurant, taking part with a pastime or relaxing evening. When you acknowledge your efforts and effort, you can create positive connections with your proactive actions.

19.2 Strategies for Preventing Regression

To prevent regression, you must take an approach that is proactive and addresses the triggers and potential pitfalls which can lead to delay. Through these techniques to strengthen your resilience, you can guard against the possibility of relapse.

Mindful Self-Awareness: Monitoring Triggers

Be mindful of your self and identify factors that led to procrastination over the years. The triggers can be anxiety, stress, fatigue, perfectionists or even an context. When you identify these triggers you can make the necessary changes to reduce their effects.

Adaptive Planning: Flexibility and Adaptability

Embrace adaptive planning. It is a dynamic world, which means situations can alter abruptly. Instead of viewing any deviations in your plans as a failure consider them opportunities to change and adapt. Flexibility can reduce anxiety and the consequent need to put off work.

Accountability Rituals: Regular Check-Ins

Set up accountability routines. Be sure to regularly review your progress as well as setbacks and goals. This method not only helps to keep you on track, but makes you accountable to yourself. The sharing of your accomplishments with a accountability partner could give an outside perspective as well as encouragement.

19.3 Cultivating a Proactive and Action-Oriented Lifestyle

Making progress on a long-term basis against procrastination doesn't have to be limited to one-off efforts. It's a lifestyle. Achieving a more proactive and active life involves integrating the principles of efficiency into your everyday routine.

Time Blocking and Routine: Anchoring Productivity

Practice time blocking regularly as well as creating routines to prioritize activities that are proactive. Consistency in your method helps you stay productive and reduces the lure of procrastination.

Learning and Growth Mindset: Embracing Challenges

Create a growth attitude. Consider challenges as opportunities to grow rather than hurdles that you must avoid. If you can frame failures as opportunities to learn You can eliminate the fear of failure which is often the reason for the habit of procrastinating.

Positive Self-Talk: Inner Dialogue of Empowerment

Make positive self-talk a habit. Change self-doubt into affirmations that boost your capabilities and resiliency. The change in your inner dialogue improves confidence and lessens your tendency to delay work because of self-limiting thoughts.

The tapestry of individual development, making steady progress when it comes to overcoming the procrastination issue is an affirmation of your determination and perseverance. Through celebrating your milestones, using strategies to avoid regression and establishing a routine that encourages action-oriented thinking, you break the chains of acceptance and move into the realm of continual development and success. As you dance between growth or stagnation are the conductor of your life by orchestrating a harmonious symphony intentional living.

Chapter 9: Embracing A Procrastination-Free Future

When we've reached the end of our journey and stand on the edge of a non-procrastination future. The road we've taken is one of discovery the power of resilience and growth. In this chapter we look back on our transformative journey, explore the fundamentals of living an existence that is full of purpose and satisfaction, and consider the impact that it has on others to let go of the binds of delay.

20.1 The Transformational Journey: Reflecting Back

When you reflect on your efforts to free yourself from the burden of the habit of procrastinating, you an image of your personal growth and progress.

The Ripple Effect of Change

Your changes has impacted all areas of your existence. The procrastinator you were has transformed to an active doer. It wasn't all about efficiency, it was about taking back your power, revising your own story and taking on the potential you have.

Lessons in Resilience and Perseverance

Reminisce about times when that you had setbacks or Relapses. These were not failures. they taught you about resilience and determination. Every stumble offered a chance to grow stronger and more determined.

20.2 Living a Life of Purpose and Fulfillment

By letting go of procrastination, we can open an opportunity to live an existence that is centered around purpose and filled with joy.

Aligned Goals and Actions

When procrastination is no longer holding on you, your priorities and activities are synchronized. It is easier to pursue goals that align with your ideals and values and are fueled by the belief that you've got the ability to turn them into reality.

Present-Moment Engagement

Procrastinating no longer is a way to allow the person to completely be in your present. Enjoy each step or conversation free of the burdensome cloud of incomplete chores. The presence of your loved ones enhances the happiness with the everyday pleasures of life.

Expanded Horizons of Possibility

Once you get rid of the burdens of procrastination, you broaden your possibilities of what's possible. The doors are opened and new abilities are cultivated as well as new goals can be pursued. Your potential to grow is limitless possibilities.

20.3 Inspirational Others to Break Free of the Cycle of Procrastination

The path you've taken is an source of hope for those struggling in the same struggle.

Leading by Example

When you lead a stress-free, procrastination-free life and setting the example, you set.

Your followers witness your progress and can see that it can be achieved. Your experience becomes a testimony to our human potential to grow.

Sharing Your Story

Your tale has the potential to connect with other people in their journeys. Through sharing your struggles as well as your triumphs and strategies offer a road map that will help those who want to free themselves from the shackles of putting off work.

Creating a Ripple of Empowerment

When you encourage other people to take on your own journeys to be procrastination free You generate a ripple of confidence. Everyone you influence is a catalyst to changes in their circles.

When we wrap up this chapter and end this book in the pursuit to get rid of delay, be aware the fact that this quest isn't an end-to-end process but rather it is a constant evolution. Your path to a stress-free future is outlined through the actions you make every single day. Now you have the tools, knowledge and attitude to live the life you want as well as fulfillment and endless possibilities. Your journey is not over, and you are an ambassador of light, showing how others can be a part of this transformative pathway.

Chapter 10: Procrastination The Art Of Delay

Procrastination, which is frequently viewed as a nemesis to productivity, is actually a highly intricate base of psychological, behavioral and art within its layers. Although the general public views that it is a debilitating characteristic, understanding the root of it will provide profound insights in human behavior as well as the intricate connection we have with the passage of time.

1. The Definition and Understanding

In essence, procrastination is the practice of putting off or putting off the completion of tasks. But, the definition only barely scratches the rough surface. There is an array of feelings, between defiance and fear, from anger to anger. Procrastination isn't only a delay of action it is a telling of internal conflict and pressures from outside.

2. The Historical View

In the past, procrastination has been criticized, mocked as well as sometimes revered. In the past, Greeks called it "akrasia" - acting against the best judgment of one's self. Philosophers such as Socrates and Aristotle thought about the reasons why people avoid actions they believe to be advantageous. The study reveals that procrastination does not exist as something that is new, but it is an ancient aspect of our human nature.

3. Psychological Underpinnings

An array of psychological triggers causes us to procrastinate. The fear of failing causes us to postpone tasks in order to defend ourselves method. There's also the paradox of choice'. The more choices we have the longer we put off making a decision which leads to procrastination of making a decision. A third factor is the instant incentive bias that makes us prioritize the pleasures of today (like watching television) ahead of future rewards (like finishing a task).

4. The Artistry in Procrastination

Procrastination being considered an art may seem odd However, there's a nitty-gritty when it comes to how we manage obligations, tasks as well as interruptions. As an artist decides which brush stroke to use next the mind of a procrastinator constantly considers the importance of each task, but sometimes not in a productive manner.

Furthermore, certain forms of procrastination are productive. It's referred to as "productive procrastination," it's the case when someone delays an activity however, instead of sitting or wasting time on a job, such as putting off an assignment to tidy the workplace. There's still a delay and is accompanied by a feeling satisfaction.

5. The Societal Impact of Delay

In an age that encourages speed and instant results Procrastinators are often viewed as a minority. However, many of the world's most innovative minds, ranging from Leonardo da

Vinci to Douglas Adams were renowned for being procrastinators. They were adamant about the art of delaying, letting ideas simmer to create incredible works. Though procrastination over and over again is harmful, even sporadic delays, when used in a responsible manner they can prove to be a great source for creative thinking.

6. Embracing and Managing the Art of Delay

Recognizing that there's a moment for action as well as a time for contemplation is vital. Learning to master the technique of procrastination is about being aware of when you should let your brain wander and knowing when it's time to stop. Methods such as the "Pomodoro" divide tasks into time periods, which allows time-bound breaks or planned procrastination, if it do.

The Clockmaker's Paradox

The late Mr. Lysander, a renowned clockmaker, was a man with a unique belief system: he believed time wasn't an entity that could be described as linear, but rather an enormous ocean of time where the time-based moments were interspersed.

An afternoon, a woman known as Ivy went to his store. "Mr. Lysander," she said, "I've been told you can craft clocks that don't just tell time but understand it."

Lysander smiledand said "Ah, you speak of my special creations. What do you seek, young lady?"

"A way to delay time," Ivy thought and her eyes were glistening with optimism. "You see, I always feel rushed, forever chasing deadlines, never savoring the present. I've missed sunsets with my loved ones and ignored spring blossoms, all because I kept pushing things for 'later.' I need time to be on my side."

Incredulous, Lysander decided to craft the perfect clock for Ivy and not any ordinary clock. The one he created wouldn't move forward, instead it will embrace each second, making it longer. The author named the thing "The Procrastinator."

When Ivy went to get her clock Ivy noticed something strange. It seemed like time was slowing. The hours seemed longer, plus they were more rich. Things she would normally rush through were now given the time to contemplate. Then she began living with each moment rather than rushing between them. The world, under the trance of the Procrastinator permitted her to breathe, to think, to take in the moment.

As the days grew into weeks, Ivy began to feel more restless. The art of delaying is beautiful but equally enticing. The woman began delaying crucial choices, focusing over the moment and not paying attention to the in the future.

In the evening, while Ivy was watching a long evening, she knew that that the equilibrium she was seeking wasn't prolonging time, but instead in harmony with the rhythm of it.

Delay has its appeal, however it was also the rhythm of progress.

Then she returned to Mr. Lysander, "Your clock is magical, but I've learned that to appreciate the present truly, I must also respect the future."

Lysander acknowledged, "The Procrastinator was not to change your essence but to show you the beauty and peril of delay."

He returned the clock and then gave Ivy an alternative. It didn't speed up time, however it had an interesting aspect: each hour past it would play with a tune that re-inforced Ivy to enjoy a time of her time.

After Ivy was gone, Lysander smiled, reminded that he was once more in the duality of the moment. It was force, an ebb and flow, or sometimes it was a deliberate delay. It was, however, more importantly it served as a guide aiding souls like Ivy to discover their own rhythm within the unending dance of time.

The art of delaying can be a double-edged weapon. Although it may hinder productivity and cause anxiety, it also can serve as a catalyst for contemplation, creative thinking and new insights. The secret lies not in elimination, but knowing and mastering. In recognizing the nuances of it and becoming able to dance in a slow motion, we is able to transform the procrastination habit from an adversary to an unexpected all-weather ally.

Chapter 11: Understanding Procrastination

Procrastination is an intricate behaviour pattern. In order to conquer it, one must know the root of it:

Procrastination: The Hidden Layers

On the surface at first glance, it could appear to be simply a reluctance or unwillingness to perform work, or a temporary lack of motivation that we all fall victim to. However, beneath the surface of this action lies a murky web of fears, emotions and conflicting needs. In order to truly tackle procrastination it is necessary to understand its root.

Fear of Failure

Many feel that the fear of failure can be far more frightening than the challenge.

The root of this fear originates from previous experiences in which initiatives led to a disappointing outcome. Past failures, in particular those that are publicly exposed or have brought to negative feedback, form an image that implies that the future or current endeavors could be the same.

Signs of Fear: Fear of Failure could manifest itself as a reluctance to start a task and a feeling of anxiety or fear in the face of work or an excessive amount of preparation, and not ever tackling the work.

Overcoming Fear of Failure:

Change the way you view failure: instead thinking of failure as a devastating conclusion, think of it as a element of learning.

Create realistic expectations Know that perfection is not attainable. Focus on progress and not perfection.

Acceptance: Embrace vulnerability. Everyone fails. The important thing is to adjust and grow.

Perfectionism

The desire to design something that is perfect could stop creation completely.

The genesis of the phenomenon: Perfectionism may develop from childhood pressures from family or academic life in which only the most successful outcomes were acknowledged, while the less than was viewed as unworthy.

Signs of a Perfectionist: They often devote an excessive amount of time focusing on small details. They struggle to think of a job as "complete," or avoid taking the first step unless they're certain that the outcome will be up to the high standards they set for themselves.

Overcoming Perfectionism:

Focus on Progress: Concentrate on the next step, even if each step isn't 100% perfect.

Time constraints: Create specific and precise time constraints for each task to avoid over-fixing.

Accept iteration as a part of the process: Know that drafts and variants can be improved on.

Decisional Procrastination

Sometimes, the challenge isn't about completing the job, but rather deciding on the best way to tackle it.

The root of this is fear of making a incorrect choice. When every decision is weighed with serious consequences, the decision can be a daunting task.

Signs of Indecisiveness: Constant investigation without conclusiveness, or looking for endless help without a plan can be signs of procrastination that is decisional.

Overcoming Decisional Procrastination:

Limit Options: Reducing options to make the process easier to manage.

The 2-Minute Rule If the time is less than two minutes, make a decision today.

Pros & Cons: Old-fashioned? Yes. Effective? Absolutely. Writing these down can help you make the decision-making process.

Task Aversion

The nature of the work itself acts as an obstacle.

The root of the problem is due to tasks that are perceived to be too difficult, time-consuming or void of intrinsic reward. The tasks aren't in line with the interests of individuals or their immediate targets.

Expression: A strong feeling of displeasure or even resentment in the face of the task deliberately seeking distractions, and reasons for what the job isn't needed.

Overcoming Task Aversion:

Break it down Then break the complex task into manageable, smaller sub-tasks.

Rewards System: Create incentives for those who complete certain aspects of the job.

Mindset shift: Develop a way to make this task seem more appealing. Could it be viewed as a test or opportunity to grow?

The Unpainted Canvas

The center of Paris in the bustling avenues of Montmartre was Eloise, a talented artist. The studio she had was charming that overlooked the square, where artists showcased their work, attracting compliments and even pennies from passersby.

One day, a renowned art dealer named Monsieur Dupont visited Montmartre. The word spread about his desire for the most unique artwork to be displayed at a major art show. Everyone in the gallery wanted to create an impression.

Eloise was able to come up with an artwork she thought would draw Dupont's attention. The painting was a stunning contrast of night and day along with the famous Eiffel Tower that spanned the two realms. However, days turned into weeks, but her canvas was never finished.

Every time she saw the painting, with a brush the feeling of overwhelming overwhelm her.

"What if I can't capture the image as perfectly as it is in my mind? What if Dupont hates it? Maybe I should wait for the right inspiration," she thought as she let her time drift off her shoulders.

A few days later, her acquaintance Rebecca was visiting. After seeing the canvas in its entirety, Rebecca inquired, "Eloise, why haven't you started your masterpiece? The exhibition is merely a week away!"

Eloise hesitated before revealing her worries "I want it to be perfect. The vision in my head is vivid and beautiful, but I'm scared I'll ruin it once I start."

Rebecca was taking a breath she picked up a small brush and dipped it into blue paint, then drew an oblique stroke across the canvas. Eloise gasped.

"There," Rebecca said smiled, "Now the canvas isn't completely perfect. However, it's still there. Your job is to transform the stroke into something stunning."

Eloise was awestruck but also inspired. was awestruck but determined to take on the challenge. She worked all day long until the final day this week her work displayed a stunning landscape. What was the blue stroke Rebecca did? It was transformed into the glistening Seine which reflected the lights of the Eiffel Tower.

Monsieur Dupont was fascinated by the work of Eloise and decided to select to exhibit it. For Eloise her greatest achievement was not the award, but in beating her relentless pursuit of excellence.

The blank canvas has taught her that often the fear of failing and imperfection is the most significant obstacle. Most of the time all it takes is just a single stroke to start.

Procrastination being viewed as just "laziness" is an oversimplification. The issue is multifaceted and rooted in our personal experiences, views and anxieties. Through understanding the root of it as well as recognizing its manifestations and armed with the right ways to tackle its unique kinds, it is possible to overcome the obstacles of procrastination, and discover ways to be productive.

Chapter 12: Instantly Stop Procrastination Technique (Ispt)

The Birth of ISPT

In today's crowded world of self-improvement and productivity, many methods promise to aid you in overcoming your procrastination. But, they all work with time and require perseverance and discipline. What happens in those instances that you require an instant boost? Enter the Instantly Stop Procrastination Technique or ISPT. It is different from the other techniques, is created to trigger instant action that propels your body from a state of inertia and into motion.

The Core Philosophy of ISPT

The heart of the operation, ISPT operates on two basic principles:

1. The power of Starting The first difficulty is usually the most difficult. When you begin the process, you will gain momentum.

2. The Mind-Body Connection: Getting involved with your body's muscles can trigger changes in your mind, which can turn fear into determination.

The Five Pillars of ISPT

1. Recognition & Ownership:

"Awareness" is the first step towards transformation.

Prior to addressing your procrastination issue, acknowledge the problem and acknowledge the fact that you are doing it. Write out or say aloud, "I am procrastinating."

2. Physical Shift:

The principle is that physical movements help to renew the stagnant mental state.

Step: When you feel like you are putting off your work and you are not feeling well, try changing your state of mind. It could be as simple as doing 10 jumping jacks in a row, going for a the stairs, walking simply standing and stretching.

3. The Five-Minute Commitment:

The principle is that starting can be the biggest obstacle. Aiming to take just five minutes will make starting easier. difficult.

Act: Take on your task for just five minutes. Most of the time when you start the task, it will continue for a long time beyond the time limit.

4. Environment Reset:

Principle: The conditions you are in could encourage procrastination, or encourage actions.

Step: Get rid of any distractions in your immediate surroundings. This may mean switching off notifications that are unnecessary, cleaning your desk, or employing headphones that enhance focus.

5. Visualize Completion:

Concept: Connecting your emotions with satisfaction at accomplishment of a task can be an effective motivator.

Act: Take an instant imagining your final stage of your life. What will be the feeling you'll have once the task is completed? How will the environment you live in change? What are the positive effects you can expect?

The ISPT in Action

We can look at a possible instance study: Alex, a writer who is struggling with writer's block.

1. Recognition and Ownership Alex admits that, "I'm avoiding writing."

2. Physical Shift Alex performs a short sequence of push-ups that gets circulation.

3. The Five-Minute Commitment. He promises, "I'll write for just five minutes." He set an alarm.

4. Setting the Environment: Alex clears his desk closes his social media, then starts his software for writing.

5. Visualize Completion: Prior to starting, Alex imagines a sense of satisfaction and relief when he has completed this chapter.

What did it produce? Alex is writing continuously for over about an hour. He broke through his blocks.

Why ISPT Works

ISPT doesn't have magic powers However, it does feel like it. Its power lies in these areas:

Interrupting Patterns ISPT can stop the downward spiral of procrastination with unexpected, sudden modifications.

Lowering entry barriers: When tasks are reduced to five minutes of work, it's easier to get started.

"Tapping into the Emotion Visualizing the completion of a task creates an emotional tug that shifts your attention from the pain of beginning to the joy of completing.

The Forgotten Presentation

Sarah who was a meticulous marketing professional, valued her pride by always being at the at the top of her game. On a Monday, she was in an unusual situation. Her mind was completely blank the presentation she was required to present before members of the Board on Wednesday. It was an important presentation on the new marketing plan, but she hadn't prepared one slide.

She sat down and stared at her screen with the blinking cursor on the blank PowerPoint screen that appeared to be mocking. She thought about the mountains of data that she had to sort through, the graphic she'd have to create as well as the time she'd need to practice. The sheer magnitude of the project overwhelmed her. When she was attempting to get started her day, she'd come up with a reason to look at her emails and make coffee or talk to a coworker. It was a slow morning until lunch time, when she wasn't even making progress.

In the meantime, she was reminded of the workshop she took part in one month ago, which introduced to the Instantly Stop Procrastination Method (ISPT). In a state of despair and unable to find alternatives She decided to try an attempt:

1. Ownership and Recognition: Sarah was able to take a breath and looked into the mirror and confessed, "I'm procrastinating big time!"

2. Physical shift The day she was not eating her regular lunch in her office She took a quick 15 minutes of walking outside. The fresh air rejuvenated her.

3. The Five-Minute Commitment: After returning to her workstation She put her timer at five minutes and then thought "I'll just outline the first section. That's all."

4. The Environment Reset feature: She set her phone in airplane mode, shut down every tab that was not related to it and put on noise-canceling headphones.

5. Visualize the completion Take a second to visualize the board's nodding heads, feeling of relief, as well as the happiness of having a job accomplished.

The moment she began, the five minutes grew into thirty after which it was an hour at the end of the day Sarah had completed the version of her pitch. The next day she spent practicing and refining her pitch before presenting on Wednesday. she gave a thorough and compelling presentation.

The audience was awed, not only by the speech, but also by Sarah's capacity to deal with the pressure. It was not known that the key to her accomplishment was a single strategy she came across as well as a promise she had made herself to only work for "five minutes."

The ISPT was not just a way to save Sarah from a bad day. Sarah and her family, but was also the first thing she used to do when she sensed the cloud of procrastination hanging over her.

In a culture that promotes strategies for long-term success and lasting determination, ISPT stands out as a lighthouse for those times that you require an instant stimulation. It's certainly not a substitute of long-term routines and discipline It's a valuable instrument for those who want to break free from the stain of putting off work for too long.

Chapter 13: Step-By-Step Guide

The waters of work aren't easy. If you use ISPT, the Instantly Stop Procrastination Method (ISPT) however it's equipped with a mooring, making sure you're not lost for long. This chapter provides an extensive guide to using ISPT and explains each step.

Step 1: Acknowledge the Act

A Theory of Change: The initial step to solving any issue is to recognize that there's only one. Before making changes, we need to be aware of our present situation.

The Application:

"Be Honest With Yourself The moment is not to excuse yourself or avoid the issue. Remind yourself that "I am procrastinating."

Note it down: write it down in your journal or in a notepad. Writing provides an actual proof that you have acknowledged your request.

Be Neutral: Stay clear of self-blame and negativity. You are allowed to delay things from time to time. Recognizing it is about understanding not criticizing.

Step 2: Break the Task

The Theory is that a daunting job is often viewed as impossible. If you break it down into smaller pieces, it can be made easier to handle and less daunting.

The Application:

Note Down the sub-tasks you need to complete: If, for instance, you're making a presentation, break the report into research, outline and edit and then finalize.

Prioritize: Determine what sub-tasks are the most important and work on them first.

Small wins: Once you accomplish each task Celebrate the small wins. This increases motivation and boosts morale.

Step 3: Immediate Action

It's the Theory: Starting is often the toughest aspect. If you commit to a mere five minutes, you'll reduce the psychological barriers that prevent people from taking on the job.

The Application:

Set a Timer Utilize a tangible timer or phone. The countdown visual creates an urgency that keeps the ability to focus.

You can make a promise to yourself: at the five-minute mark and you're not sure if you want to stop, you may. In reality, more often or not, you'll be going on.

"Embrace the Momentum If the ball has started to roll and you can keep it going. Following the initial five minutes, you can determine whether you're able to dedicate additional time.

Step 4: Eliminate Distractions

The Theory: The environment we live in has a significant impact on our performance. An uncluttered and distracting space could increase the likelihood of the tendency to delay.

The Application:

Physical Space: Clean your work space. Take out any papers that are not related and close any tabs that are not needed as well as ensure that you have everything you need to complete your job.

Digital Distractions: Turn off social media notifications, put your phone on "Do Not Disturb" mode, or use apps like "Focus@Will" to play concentration-boosting music.

Mindspace: Prior to getting started, take some deep breaths, or take a moment to meditate. In clearing your mind, you set the scene for your focus.

5. Reconnect with your core purpose.

Theories: Understanding the motive of an act is an effective motivational factor. By reliving this, you can increase the enthusiasm and motivation for completing the project.

The Application:

Imagine the final goal When you're doing your homework to pass the exam, think about passing it. When you're working on a task and you're not sure how it will go, imagine its success as well as the awards that could accompany the achievement.

Affirmations: Remind yourself why the task you are doing is important. The reason could be as significant in terms of career development or as basic as your satisfying yourself.

The Ripple Effect: Be aware of that completing this project will positively impact other aspects in your work or life.

Jamie's Garden

Jamie always wanted an idyllic garden that could be an envy to her neighbours and the tranquility she's always wanted. Yet, in the midst of her career and the rigors of everyday life, she couldn't seem to make moment. Each weekend, she would look at her garden and envision the perfect garden, only to be overwhelmed by the enormity of the job. Overgrown weeds and empty patches and inexperience of knowing the best place to begin forced her to postpone the task.

After months of inactivity, Jamie stumbled upon an article on the ISPT technique. In a moment of inspiration She decided to try these steps to create her dream gardening venture:

Step 1: Acknowledge the Act:

As she sat on her front porch watching the yard in disarray She mumbled to herself, "I've been procrastinating. It's time to change that."

Step 2: Break the Task:

She took out a notebook and started jotting down her tasks.

1. Get rid of any weeds.

2. Layout the arrangement.

3. Plants and seeds can be purchased.

4. Plants and water.

Step 3: Immediate Action:

Jamie established a timer for five minutes and put on her gloves and started pulling the grass. It was surprising that when her alarm went off she became so engaged that she was unable to go on. A few hours later the majority of her yard was completely weed-free.

Step 4: Eliminate Distractions:

Her phone was sure to cause distractions with all the messages. Therefore, she decided to leave it at home. To make her task easier, she listened to the station she adores, to let the music inspire her enthusiasm.

5. Reconnect to the reason you are here:

When she was exhausted or thought of abandoning her work, Jamie would imagine her beautiful garden - vibrant flowers moving with the breeze with the fragrance of fresh blooms, the sounds of birds as well as the satisfaction of completing her task. It was this vision that kept her going.

At the close the month, Jamie's vision of a garden had become an actuality. Friends would drop by to express their appreciation for her work as her garden became an oasis of peace following a tiring day. As she reflected on her experience it was clear that what had been an daunting task was now manageable taking a methodical procedure. Every time she sip your morning cup of coffee amid the blooms, she thanked the easy but powerful actions of ISPT that turned the dream of hers into a reality.

Chapter 14: Tools And Resources To Support

In this age of digital change and digital transformation, we're blessed with numerous tools and resources that can increase our efficiency. The ISPT approach gives us a strong method to overcome procrastination the integration of technology tools will further simplify the process. This chapter offers a collection of applications and platforms which can be used to enhance the effectiveness of the ISPT technique and increase its effectiveness.

1. Timer Apps

The theory: Timer applications provide a visual representation of time that creates a feeling of urgency and determination. They give you structured breaks for focus, and provide periodic breaks to prevent burning out.

The Application:

Forest: This innovative application gamifies your the focus. Once you have set a date that you set, you can plant a tree. When you leave the app or become lost, your tree is cut down. In time, you will grow a tree, demonstrating the dedication you have shown.

How to utilize ISPT Start by setting the timer for you to meet your "Immediate Action" commitment, for example, 5 minutes. Then observe your tree growing as you get to work.

Pomodoro Technique Tools: Based on the Pomodoro Technique, these tools recommend 25-minute intervals of work (called "Pomodoros") followed by five-minute breaks.

How to utilize ISPT: Following the initial commitment of 5 minutes you can then switch into Pomodoro sessions to keep your momentum.

2. Task Managers

The theory The Theory: Task managers plan your work, making sure you're conscious of the things that require attention. They do this by visualizing tasks. they give clarity and order.

The Application:

Trello: a system based on cards which is ideal for visually-oriented people. Create boards to organize projects or cards for tasks as well as use checklists, labels and deadline dates.

What to do with ISPT in step "Break the Task" step make the Trello board to organize your overall task, and sub-tasks on cards. Once you've finished each one step, you can move it into a "Done" column, visualizing the process.

Todoist: A list of tasks checklist app that works with several platforms. It lets you define due dates, prioritizes as well as integrate into your schedule.

What to do with ISPT for any major task, make the project using "Todoist." Under it are the tasks that you have subordinated. Make deadlines, and review these each day.

3. Mental Well-being Tools

The Theory that procrastination is an outcome of fears, anxiety or anxiety. If we can address the health of our minds it is possible to tackle the issue of procrastination from the source.

The Application:

Headspace is a meditation app which offers guided meditation sessions covering a variety of topics, ranging including stress, focus and sleeping. The app is designed to be used by new and experienced practitioners.

What to do the ISPT method: Prior to getting into work or undertaking, particularly if you're anxious, consider taking the time to sit and meditate with Headspace. The "Focus" sessions are perfect for combining with the ISPT technique.

Sam's Digital Reinforcement

Being a writer who freelanced, Sam had the freedom to decide on his working time. With great freedom came the responsibility of a great deal, and recently, Sam was drowning in delay. The deadlines were always hanging over his head He was stuck, and in no position to end the vicious cycle of delay and frantic panic of the last minute.

As the user sat idly browsing through his Facebook feeds, hoping to avoid the daunting task of writing an article the post popped up on the ISPT method. Incredulous, he began to research and eventually, he was eager to test it. However, after analyzing his past performance He realized that he required more push.

It was at this point that he began to integrate tools into the ISPT process:

Timer Applications: Sam decided to download Forest. The concept of planting trees which would be destroyed if Sam got distracted was both entertaining and useful. The app was combined with an ISPT's "Immediate Action" step. If he was ever prompted to delay his work, he'd create the tree for 5 minutes.

Most of the time the time, he would be absorbed and be more productive while watching his tree grow in conjunction with the efficiency of his work.

Task Managers: To manage the writing assignments the writer made use of Trello. The boards were created with each client, and cards for each article. Feeling the satisfaction of moving the card between "In Progress" to "Completed" following the completion of an article felt like something he was looking for. It was visually a representation of progress which made the idea of the work a reality.

Mental Well-being Tools there were times when things weren't always so good. On some days, worry and doubts over Sam's own self-worth weighed heavily on his mind. In these instances, prior to beginning work, he would open Headspace. The meditation guided sessions particularly those that specifically focused on concentration and anxiety allowed him to get back into his place in the world. They also served as a cleansing of the mind, removing the burden of negativity and stress.

After a month of this routine Then, not but Sam regularly meeting deadlines but the work was being submitted days before. The clients were impressed by the increase in his punctuality, as well as an improvement in the standard of his written work. Combining the ISPT framework and digital tools has transformed his daily life.

In a meet-up for freelancers, after a fellow member was asking him about his recent changes in attitude to work, Sam smiled and said, "I've just made technology my accountability partner."

Although the ISPT offers a solid system to combat procrastination the use of the latest tools and resources will improve your results. The apps don't just support this method, but they also respond to your the individual's preferences. This ensures that you're not only performing hard work, but you're also making smart decisions When you begin your path to defeating procrastination use technology as your partner in accelerating your work and helping you make progress faster.

Chapter 15: Common Pitfalls And How To Overcome Them

The issue of procrastination, although a constant problem, isn't an all-encompassing problem you'll have to face in your way to becoming productive. If you implement strategies such as ISPT to combat delays and resentment, you could be entangled by different obstacles. In this chapter, we dive into common traps by examining their causes and, more importantly giving strategies to get through these.

1. Overplanning

The issue is when you devote an inordinate amount of time planning or strategizing, instead of actually doing. This is like reading about methods to swim for months and not actually getting in the pool.

The Solution:

1. Set Specific Goals Before beginning to plan make a list of what you'd like to accomplish. By having a defined end-point will make it less

likely for you to get lost in the maze of over-prepared.

Limit the time for planning Decide on a set period of time to plan. If, for instance, you're making plans for a new project, put the time for a certain period of time, or day in which you will stick to the.

Action to Take Utilize the ISPT technique. Make a commitment to only five minutes of actions following the planning. Most of the time, getting started is the toughest phase. When you are in motion, your energy of the motion propels your forward.

2. Waiting for the "Right Time"

The Issue: The idea that there's a right time to do everything could be a numbing thought. In the waiting room for the right stars to align prior to taking action typically will result in missed opportunities and an increase in anxiety.

The Solution:

Challenge your Beliefs Question yourself the reason you're putting off your decision. Do you have a legitimate reason or an excuse to cover up something else?

Begin small Don't wait for the right time to kick off your new routine, begin by implementing a simple version now. If, for instance, you'd like to get started working out, do not wait until the next Monday. Take a few minutes of stretching or even a walk.

Celebrate immediate action Each time you take action immediately, without having to wait until an "right time," reward yourself. In time, it reinforces your habit of prompt decision.

3. Self-negotiation

The Issue It's the inner negotiation that occurs as you prepare to begin the task. Ideas like "If I finish this task now, I can watch an extra episode of my favorite show tonight," could be motivating, but in reality they cause delay that isn't needed.

The Solution:

Recognize the Act In the same way as with the initial step in the ISPT process to recognize the moment you're entering self-negotiating. Being aware is only half the battle.

Set boundaries If you're trying to get an 30 minutes of sleep each morning, you must be able to establish routines. In other words, you should establish that, no matter what happens it is, you'll get out of the bed before 7 AM.

Reconnect to Your Purpose As with the last part of ISPT Remind yourself of the bigger reason for doing this. What is the reason you are performing this work? What is the benefit? It can reduce the need to bargain.

Susan's Illusion of Preparation

Susan always dreamed of owning her own bakery. All of her family members and circle of close friends was aware about the dream. They'd been hearing about her meticulous plans: the rustic interior, the scent of freshly baked croissants lingering in the air, and also the creative fusion recipes she planned to showcase. Susan was "planning" her bakery for more than a decade.

Each year, at any gathering, conversations was always geared towards her goal as she updated the group with more specific information. The meticulously designed business plans, sites, ideas for marketing as well as other. The bakery, however, remained undiscovered. A common joke within the household was " Susan's been baking her bakery idea for years now!"

A few days ago, as she was enjoying a cup of coffee with her college buddy Annette, Susan started discussing her bakery. Annette had heard the story many times and asked her a very simple inquiry: " Susan, when will I be tasting your croissants instead of hearing about them?"

Susan was initially a bit sarcastic and then Annette kept going, and emphasized the three traps Susan was unaware of falling in to.

1. The overplanning Susan was more focused on refining her plan that the vast majority of others who implement their plans. Annette said the importance of planning, however there was also the thing as overplanning that became a method to avoid.

2. In the process of waiting to find an "Right Time": Susan always had a reason for her put off. There was a lack of market or she was waiting on an item to be sold or to make a bit more cash first. Annette told her that if sat looking until the sun aligned they could be awe-inspiring for a lifetime.

3. Self-negotiated: Each time Susan began to feel nervous regarding her goal and her future, she would negotiate a compromise with herself. "If I take this job now, I'll save enough to start my bakery next year," or "Maybe I should take another baking course first." Annette was aware of that Susan was using this strategy to protect herself in order to stave away the risk of following an ambition.

This evening brought a lot of joy for Susan. Annette's open and honest comments were her wake-up signal. Instead of waiting for an "sign," Susan took the first steps towards her goal. In just a few months and a half, the community witnessed the grand opening " Susan 's Confections." What about the croissants? They were as delicious as the stories she had told.

The journey to realizing this was not without its challenges, but each time Susan confronted a problem she recalled that night with Annette. Instead of returning to the old habits, she chose the path of action instead of endlessly planning in the present over the future as well as self-negotiation over commitment.

Chapter 16: Strengthening Your Willpower And Discipline

Willpower and discipline are usually considered to be natural traits that you have either you do or do not. But in actuality these are more akin to muscles. As you work them, the better they get. Although techniques such as ISPT can provide immediate relief from procrastination developing willpower and discipline is the key to longevity in all endeavors.

1. Start Small: Consistency Over Intensity

The issue: The thrill of launching a new venture or habit can lead us to establish grand big objectives. Although it is good to be ambitious however, putting too much pressure on yourself at beginning can result in burnout and discontent.

The Solution:

Mini Habits: In lieu of setting a goal for exercising for an hour every day begin with just ten minutes. This less-important goal can create positive feedback, strengthening the habit.

Develop Gradually When you're confident and the muscle of discipline strengthens Gradually increase the challenges. With this steady process, you'll be never overwhelmed and you're not stagnating.

Recognize Consistency: Although significant milestones are essential be sure to appreciate your commitment. A month filled with unbroken routines can be just as satisfying as achieving your target.

2. Reward System: Positive Reinforcement Works

The problem is that depending solely on the intrinsic motivation of your employees can cause exhaustion. With no tangible results at the beginning It's not difficult to doubt the effectiveness of your work.

The Solution:

Set Milestones: Split your travel into manageable points. When you have reached one, give yourself a reward.

Rewards that are tangible: Although being satisfied with a task accomplished is an incentive sometimes, giving yourself something tangible (like the food you love or a good book) could be a great way to motivate yourself.

Beware of rewards that can be counterproductive. If you'd like to stick to healthy eating habits, don't indulge in junk food. Make sure that your rewards align with, or don't hinder your main goals.

3. Accountability Partner: Shared Goals and Collective Strength

The problem is that working on your own can be a drain on motivation. There's nobody to talk about your successes or struggles with which can lead to an absence of perspective from outside.

The Solution:

Select wisely The person you choose to be your accountability partner must be someone who really wants for you to succeed, and doesn't hesitate to offer constructive feedback.

Check-ins on a regular basis Schedule periodic review sessions with your companion. Discussion of your experiences by sharing stories, experiences as well as gaining insight are extremely beneficial.

Use Peer Pressure positively The knowledge that someone else is interested in your dreams could give you that boost in moments when you're weak.

Lucas and the Symphony of Discipline

Lucas has always been attracted to the fascinating world of music, especially the cello. When he turned 25 Lucas decided to purchase the instrument and begin learning to play. Imagines of impressing people with his performances filled his thoughts. The reality was a hammer blow. The cello isn't an instrument that was easy to master And he had a hard time with even the most basic of notes.

Begin Small: Embarrassed by the complexity of the piece, Lucas decided to reassess. Instead of attempting to play complete pieces, he focused in gaining mastery of one scale at one time. Each day after work, he would dedicate fifteen minutes of practice to improve the bowing and finger placement techniques for the scale he was working on.

Rewards System In order to keep his motivation to keep the fire burning, Lucas promised himself rewards to celebrate his small achievements. Each time he mastered a scale and mastered, he could reward himself with a trip to a local jazz venue or purchase a brand new instrument. The rewards he received became milestones encouraging him to improve each scale, note and eventually, the complete music composition.

Accountability Partner Lucas has shared his journey in music with his best friend Cindy the pianist. Cindy became his sounding board. They started weekly classes during which Lucas presented his knowledge, and then, in turn, Cindy would play the piano. These meetings, full of positive feedback, laughter as well as a few moments of sheer anger, turned into the high points of Lucas the week. The knowledge that Cindy is waiting to hear about his achievements was a sign of trust which he had not anticipated.

As the months grew into decades, Lucas's dedication borne results. Lucas was no longer a newbie struggling with the scales. The cellist was a regular at local shows and captivated audiences with his passion and proficiency.

The experience has taught Lucas that dreams can't be realized in a single day. It was his consistent, little steps, the excitement of a reward, and the bonding with Cindy which turned his idea into an enthralling life. It wasn't all focused on notes, it was a concerto of commitment, discipline and unflinching determination.

Beginning small, and maintaining regularity, making use of rewards for motivation and bringing someone to help you along the way You'll be equipped with a an effective toolkit. By using these methods that you'll be able to not only face through the obstacles ahead, but establish the basis for lasting accomplishment in any future ventures.

In order to build willpower and discipline, it is knowing your psyche, creating support systems and routinely taking stock and revising. Although it may be difficult however, the result is transformative. Through improved determination, not only will you accomplish your objectives and objectives, but your entire experience is more satisfying and enjoyable.

Chapter 17: Success Stories Real-Life Implementations

All over the world, people have to contend with the habit of procrastination, regardless professional, age or background. There are many who have found comfort with this technique Instantly stop procrastination technique (ISPT) and have made breakthroughs. This chapter details the transformative experiences of four people who utilized the power of ISPT.

1. Angela: The Entrepreneur

At the age of 30, Angela dreamed of starting a clothing line that was sustainable. However, with a full-time work and family responsibilities Her dream was continually abandoned. The magnitude of her dream caused her to be apathetic, constantly looking for that perfect timing.

Upon discovering ISPT, Angela's mindset shifted. She recognized her procrastination, and rearranged her huge task into smaller ones. Angela began by dedicating only five minutes each day to market study. In the process of removing distractions the five minutes grew to several hours. Angela always kept herself focused on the "why," visualizing a future where sustainable fashion would benefit the world.

The brand of Angela is not just a new brand, but is also making waves on the sustainable fashion scene, all due to the organized approach of ISPT.

2. Robert: The Aspiring Novelist

Robert always longed to write the novel of his dreams, but never beyond the initial chapter. When he would sit at his desk to write, doubts about himself came in and made him think and write again, while stuck in a never-ending loop.

Finding ISPT was an important crucial turning point. Robert started by recognizing the patterns of his procrastination. Instead of attempting to write down an entire masterpiece in a single sitting He shattered the writing process. By committing to writing just 5 minutes a day and he was often engaged throughout the day. Robert employed apps to get rid of distracting factors and constantly remind himself of his love for telling stories.

One year later Robert's debut novel landed on the bookshelves, which is a testimony to the strength of organized focused effort.

3. Michelle: The Student

Michelle is a student at college often found herself studying in the evening before her examinations, which resulted in stress and low marks. The amount of syllabus she had to study was too much for her and she was forced to hold off studying to the very last moment.

Then, Michelle stumbled upon ISPT. Michelle began to recognize her habit of cramming for exams at the last minute. Utilizing this method of dividing her curriculum into smaller chunks that could be managed. In a pledge to only study 5 minutes on a single topic but soon realized that getting started at the beginning was the most difficult part. By putting her smartphone in airplane mode, removing distractions, and a clear understanding of her goals in school, Michelle transformed her study practices.

What does it mean? High marks and an improved knowledge of her subject, due to ISPT.

4. Leo: The Fitness Enthusiast

Leo was a member of the most popular gym around, however his participation was minimal at the best. The idea of an hour's hard workout was a bit intimidating.

When Leo discovered about ISPT He began at a low level. Leo started with acknowledging his resistance and decided to divide the workout down into smaller pieces. In committing to only 5 minutes at first and then he would find him working out for hours. While his workout clothes were set up the night prior to avoid distractions, and with having a clear idea of the goals he wanted to achieve Leo's determination to be fit was unabated.

Not just is Leo more fit, but he is also a participant in sports events that are held locally that inspire others on the way.

Monica and the Art of Mosaic Creation

Monica who was a middle school teacher of art, has always been fascinated by mosaics. It was the intricate process of creating pictures using small pieces of stained glass, stones or any other material. It was fascinating to see how small pieces of material could be put together into a stunning as well as a cohesive piece. In the past, she had a dream of creating a huge-scale mosaic on the exterior walls of the art facility, however the scale of the undertaking was always intimidating.

In a peaceful Sunday when she was browsing on a forum online, Monica stumbled upon a discussion on the ISPT. Incredulous, she researched further and then decided to use this technique to her ideal project.

Confirming her inclination to put off the work due to the size of it, she made the announcement in the monthly school newsletter her plan to make the mosaic. The entire school was being aware of the project, she experienced an increased sense of dedication.

To help break down the work, Monica started with designing an uninvolved portion of the mural. She sketched out designs, before settling on the palette of colors. Monica promised herself that she would take just 5 minutes each morning to set up a few pieces and often found that when she began it was hard to end her work.

To keep the distractions at bay to keep her focus on the art, she created the space as an space for art, with all of her objects in order and accessible. In the course of weeks, days it began taking form. Each time she was stressed, Monica would reconnect with her "why," thinking of the excitement and joy that the final mural could be able to bring her students.

A few months later, a lively mosaic was completed and transformed the previously dull wall into a work of art that told the story of creativity as well as the power of beginning with a small amount. Monica's experience was not only concerned with creating art, but it was an example of the strength of dedication and the value of everyday discipline, as well as the transformational power of the ISPT.

Each story demonstrates one common thread that is the potential of beginning with a small, structured. In the same way that ISPT gives a foundation but the individual stories through the lives of Angela, Robert, Michelle and Leo demonstrate the individuality of conquering the habit of putting off work. Their experiences provide a source of hope for those looking to end the cycle of inaction and dithering.

Chapter 18: Frequently Asked Questions

It is said that the Instantly Stop Procrastination technique (ISPT) has been gaining a lot of attention because many people have reported it to be efficient in tackling procrastination. But, like any method, there are questions about the adaptability, utility as well as its effectiveness in a variety of situations. In this article, we will address some of the frequently requested questions regarding ISPT.

1. Can ISPT be used in longer-term projects?

Answer: Absolutely! ISPT is highly adaptable and is able to be used for short-term and lengthy projects. The principle of ISPT is its capacity to prompt action and break the stalemate of delay. For long-term projects:

Accept the Act Accept the possibility of delaying your project due to the nature of its long-term nature. Recognizing this is the initial step to address the issue.

Break down the task: Break the project down into milestones or phases. Each phase is a mini-project, and then divide it into the daily and weekly assignments.

Immediate action: By focusing your attention only on the smaller or less important tasks stages, you could use the concept of putting aside just five minutes for starting. In most cases, beginning is the most difficult aspect.

Remove distractions and reconnect to Your Purpose Like any other task maintaining a tidy space and always keeping your mind focused on the final purpose keeps you focused.

When you chunk a project that is long-term by following ISPT, you can create the appearance of a short-term series of work that make the project more easy to handle and less overwhelming.

2. What can you do to keep momentum going after the initial phase of ISPT?

Answer: Though ISPT is a fantastic instrument for launching a project but maintaining the momentum is important. How can you keep the momentum going:

Set clear milestones You should mark certain milestones for your work or project. Be proud of these little wins. This gives you a feeling of achievement.

Regularly Review: Spend the time every week to review your progress. Make adjustments to your plans if you need.

Visual Aids: Develop an image of your progress. This could be charts or calendars. The process of seeing your progress is extremely motivating.

Keep in touch with your Motive: Constantly keep in mind the purpose of your project or task. This acts like a compass, helping you through times of doubt or exhaustion.

3. Do I have the ability to use ISPT to help with group projects or assignments?

Yes, ISPT is modified to be used in group work using a couple of modifications:

Group acknowledgement Start with a group meeting in which everyone is aware of the significance of the job and also the difficulties or obstacles that must be overcome.

Task delegation As you would split a project for one person, break your group project into separate duties or assignments. Make sure that each participant knows what their role is.

Take immediate action in a Group: Schedule a "kick-off" session in which everybody commits just a little bit of time for starting the process. It creates a sense of collective energy.

Check-ins on a regular basis In order to avoid any distractions and to ensure that everyone's on the same page Make sure you have regular check-ins and the progress meetings.

Connect with the group's purpose: Talk about and keep in mind the significance of the task. The knowledge that you're a in the middle of something bigger and that the team is dependent on you is an effective motivator.

While it's a basic approach, its value is in its flexibility. It doesn't matter if you're working by yourself or in a group or whether it's a single day's assignment or a whole year's worth of work ISPT could be the way to break through the shackles of procrastination, and moving into a realm filled with action and achievement.

Chapter 19: The Path Forward

Procrastination as we've traversed its tangled pathways it is both a threat as well as a sporadic friend. Its origins are in the mix of emotions and cognitive prejudices and social pressures. As we are on the brink of knowing, a new perspective awaits us - one that is without the burdens of ineffective delay but filled with reverence for the slow pauses which sometimes life demands.

1. Recognizing the Balance

Any effort to stop the habit of procrastination starts with a sense of the concept of balance. Procrastination at its root it is the result of an imbalance between the past and future, between action as well as the inaction. As we've seen there aren't all delays that are negative. In some cases, delay can be beneficial. But the real problem, in this case it is not to get rid of the delay, but rather to understand the use of it.

2. Redefining Procrastination

Instead of seeing procrastination as a problem It might be better to view it as a message. Our mind is communicating something to us. It could be that the job you're working on doesn't match with our beliefs or perhaps we're inadequately prepared to tackle this task at present. When we are able to recognize these signals, and knowing the source of these signals, we are able to tackle our jobs with greater focus and clarity.

3. Creating a Blueprint for Action

The transition from delaying to action is much easier if there is a plan. The blueprint must include:

Achieving Clear Goals: Knowing exactly the direction you're heading to eliminates doubt.

Prioritization: Not every job requires your attention immediately. Differentiate between urgent and the crucial.

Chunking: Divide the tasks into smaller pieces so that you don't feel overwhelmed.

Planned Breaks: Give some time to reflect and relax and rest, making them element of the program instead of a source of distraction.

4. Cultivating a Proactive Mindset

It is essential to change your mindset. Develop a positive attitude that lets you are in control of your work, rather than taking them under your control. It's not just about reacting to the world, but is seeking to change the world around it.

5. Continuous Learning and Adaptation

Procrastination and its battle against it continues. As we mature and change as do our tasks as well as our goals and obstacles. Being committed to our personal development as well as being open to the latest methods and ideas will help make sure we are in front of the game and avoid procrastination.

6. Building a Support System

Begin to surround yourself with those who can understand your needs and will be there to help you on your progress. This can take the in the form of mentors, accountability partners or similar communities. Sharing victories and challenges can make the journey much easier and fulfilling.

7. Celebrate Progress, Not Just Outcomes

Finally, don't forget to celebrate those small victories. It is important to recognize that progress can be made by small steps and every one step taken away from putting off work and to productivity is an accomplishment. The recognition and reward you receive for the accomplishments you have achieved boosts your enthusiasm.

The Library of Tomorrow

It was once a grand library dubbed"the Library of Tomorrow. It was unlike any other library. it didn't have old books or those from current. It was instead home to a myriad of books that were yet to be written and stories that were yet to be shared, and new knowledge that is still to be explored.

Penelope was a brilliant writer who often was a frequent visitor to this quaint place. The reason she went was not to read but to think. Every time she entered the room, she'd look at the blank page that had her name embossed across the cover. This was symbolic of her dream of the book she would write "someday."

The librarian, an old woman by the name of Eliza has been watching Penelope for a long time. She was observant of the way Penelope came in, stare intently at the book, then walk away with a wistful musing of the ideal plot, appropriate mood, or just waiting for an idea.

The other day, when Penelope was heading out, Eliza called out to her "Why does your book remain empty, dear child?"

Penelope smiled and said, "I want to write, but it's never the right time. There's always something that keeps me from starting."

Eliza called Penelope closer, and she whispered "The Library of Tomorrow holds the potential of the future. But remember, tomorrow is crafted by what you do today."

She gave Penelope the quill with its feathers glistening with the peculiar light. "This is the Quill of Now," Eliza declared. "Whatever you write with it takes form immediately. But there's a catch: it only works if you start immediately. Delay and its magic fades."

Penelope did not want to be seen but, determinedly, she began to open her journal. She started writing with her quill, which was dancing around the pages. Days turned into hours, and before long, her blank book was filled with stories of distant places, heroic deeds and unending affection.

When the final word was written in the library, it lit up with glowing with a gold glow that surrounded each shelf and showcasing an epic tale that was brought to life.

Penelope discovered the truth: The moment she'd long awaited did not lie in the far future, but rather the present moment she made. It was clear that The Quill of Now was merely one tool. The real power was in the beginning.

The following day, Penelope became a beacon for everyone who came to The Library of Tomorrow. The story of Penelope was an ode to the notion that the road to success from the rat race is to take swift action and not awaiting for that elusive "perfect time'.

As for The Library of Tomorrow, it was timeless and a constant reminder that even though tomorrow has unlimited possibilities, the ability to make it happen lies with the people who take action today.

www.ingramcontent.com/pod-product-compliance
Lightning Source LLC
Chambersburg PA
CBHW071446080526
44587CB00014B/2007